D1592124

What coaches are saying about Terry Geurkink's *Tennis Training Games and Tips for Ambitious Coaches, Players, and Parents*

This is an outstanding book that covers every phase of our great game, and it fills a need for both players and coaches.

The individual player will find helpful tips, coaches will discover suggested structures for team practices, and players and coaches will have a vast selection of drills and games to choose from, to add to their daily routine.

My congratulations and thanks to Terry for his time and effort in making this book available to all of us involved in the great game of tennis.

John Powless
Owner and Director of the John Powless Tennis Center, Madison, Wisconsin. Holder of 32 World Titles in singles, doubles, and team championships. Has coached players who have won Grand Slams, Davis Cups, Federation Cups, who have been World #1 Ranked open and junior players. Member of 8 Hall of Fames, including tennis and basketball.

Terry understands the complexities of the game and sport of tennis. His book is a rich resource for high school coaches teaching the game, and for parents whose kids are learning the game.

The competitive and cooperative games are fun, innovative, and productive. The author gives many tips that serve as teaching and learning tools. Many of his views and philosophies about tennis are also valuable life lessons.

I believe this book will be used and appreciated by all tennis enthusiasts.

Brian Fleishman
Head Coach, University of Wisconsin-Madison Women's Tennis

I've known Terry via contact at Madison-area tennis events over the past 15 years. His passion for tennis is unmatched, and his book presents refreshing and original perspectives. As a tennis parent, coach, and player, he uses his experiences to promote training players in a positive learning environment.

He has created games that incorporate today's tennis ideas and uses these to efficiently and effectively train high school players. His emphasis on competitive drilling and games to simulate match situations and match pressure is right on the money. Competitive games that isolate specific segments of match play and require multiple repetitions of specific shots are the perfect way to train players to master anticipation and ball-reading skills.

High school coaches will definitely benefit from using the book's drills and games designed to maximize quality touches in the practice setting with many players and limited coaches and courts. Coaches will appreciate attention to two facets of tennis that are often ignored: return of serve and strength and conditioning (which can often be done right on the courts).

The author's experiences as a parent and a coach make the book a must read for tennis parents whose child plays junior tournaments. The Dos and Don'ts section for tennis parents provides valuable insights and advice.

Frank Barnes
PTR Tennis Professional, University of Wisconsin-Whitewater Head Men's and Women's Tennis Coach, Director of the Warhawk Tennis Camps, Former Tennis Coach at Madison West HS, Former pro at Nakoma and Cherokee Country Clubs

When I first met Terry, it was clear to me that he was a student of the game, and this book demonstrates his passion for tennis.

It is a wonderful resource for coaches and players on multiple levels. It offers fresh takes and approaches to working with novices, as well as ideas to develop intermediate and advanced players.

For tennis parents, there are many helpful pointers to guide them through new experiences and difficult decisions.

The book is easy to read with abundant tips and suggestions for coaches, players, and parents. It will be a solid addition to the tennis enthusiast's library.

Doanh Wang
Head Coach, Men's and Women's Tennis, Colby College, Maine
Former Assistant Coach, University of Wisconsin Women's Tennis
Former Head Coach, Edgewood College Women's Tennis

As a full-time teaching professional, I spend a good part of my life thinking about all things tennis—mechanics of strokes, tactics of a singles point, the psychology and mental components of the game, movement and conditioning, doubles strategy, pre-match rituals—anything I can consider to give my players an edge. It can be all-consuming; yet in reading Terry's book, I find that an ER physician has enough love and knowledge of the game to put together a tremendous training guide not just for players and coaches but also for parents.

The information in Terry's book is excellent in content and delivery. Clearly it's the product of a long journey through day-to-day involvement with high school practices. The topics Terry addresses and the solutions he suggests are pertinent and well thought out. He is thorough in his explanations and offers helpful diagrams to illustrate his drills. This book is an easy read and can be used as a reference for years to come.

While I found the entire book helpful, I particularly liked the section for parents of tennis players. Regardless of their experience or lack thereof, many parents are unsure how to handle the foray of their children into tennis. Terry does a wonderful job of outlining the perils of this role and makes strong suggestions on how they can maintain a good relationship with their children through the process. It's a section I will be sure to point to parents in the future.

Tom Chorney
USPTA Certified Head Professional/
Director of Tennis, Cherokee Country Club,
Madison, Wisconsin

As a former high school tennis coach, I truly appreciate the methods Terry has devised to help all levels of players improve. He clearly and concisely discusses and describes techniques, tactics, and games to aid high school coaches as they train their players.

I am a relatively new tennis parent, and the book helps guide me on the tennis journey my son and I have begun to travel.

As a USTA league player, I have used many of the book's competitive games to improve.

Terry's passion for the sport of tennis is apparent throughout the book, and I am confident it will aid coaches, players, and parents in their pursuit of tennis excellence.

Pete Christofferson
Head Boys Tennis Coach, Verona Area
High School, Verona, Wisconsin, with
more than 125 dual wins, 6 conference
titles, and 3 team state appearances,
reaching the semi-finals once. Head Girls
Tennis Coach, Verona Area HS, with more
than 100 dual wins, 6 conference titles
and 2 state team appearances.

I have known Terry for several years, primarily from coaching against him. This spring, he joined our team as a volunteer assistant coach, and I had the pleasant experience of coaching with him. Our team had a phenomenal season.

This book exemplifies his passion for tennis and his creativity in teaching the game. It's a fresh approach to coaching and includes innovative approaches for maximizing player touches. It also includes many original training games to help players learn tactics, such as The Vertical Game, and The Horizontal Game. His views on "dead ball training" vs. "live ball training" in Chapter 2 are worth the price of the book. This book will improve your coaching, playing, and tennis parenting.

If you are a tennis coach in my conference, please do *not* read this book because I want to use these methods and approaches to beat your team next season! Selfishness aside, this book will elevate your coaching skills. If you are not lucky enough to have Terry as an assistant coach for your team next year, at least you will have his book.

Ben Conklin
Head Boys Tennis Coach (12 years)
Oregon High School, Oregon, WI
USPTR Certified Tennis Instructor
Former College Tennis Player

Tennis Training Games and Tips
For Ambitious Coaches, Players, and Parents

Terry Geurkink

Sugar River Press
Verona, Wisconsin

Copyright © 2013 by Terry Geurkink. All rights reserved. Printed in the United States of America. Except as permitted under the United States Copyright Act of 1976, no part of this publication may be reproduced or distributed in any form or by any means, or stored in a database or retrieval system, without the prior written permission of the publisher.

ISBN 978-0-9802237-9-8

Editorial and production services provided by CWL Publishing Enterprises, Inc., Madison, WI, www.cwlpub.com.

Cover photo by John Woods.

**This book is dedicated to our family
and to the memory of our daughter
Jenni and son Kyle**

Son Tim, grandson Graham, son-in-law Rob Tipton,
daughter Nina Tipton, wife Sally, the author, and daughter Chelsey

Contents

Contents

Contents

Contents

Preface

I have been enamored with books since a young age, and I've often contemplated writing one, but up until now did not have the passion or material to do so. Last November, our daughter Nina and I were chatting about tennis, and I was giving her information about tennis training games that I had recently created. She exclaimed, "Dad, you should write a book!" and indeed, I realized that I did have the material and passion to do so, and I started this book the same day.

My motivation to write this book includes a desire to pass on some tennis ideas and knowledge to other coaches, players, and parents and to pass on some tennis insights to our three children and son-in-law Rob, as well as to grandson Graham (who may one day pick up a racquet), and other grandchildren who may appear.

Our three adult children, Nina, Chelsey, and Tim, all got interested in tennis at ages 11 and 12, and when they did, I did also. After many years of playing casually, I became a student of the game and put in many hours learning, practicing, and playing competitive tennis. I also watched amateur and pro matches and read tennis books. When I became an assistant high school tennis coach nine years ago, I began to use my emergency medical training to help players improve. I would observe our team's players in matches, diagnose problems and weaknesses, and then devise improvement plans to use during practices when working with the players. I often spent hours, days, and sometimes weeks creating training approaches and games that could benefit our players. This book is a compilation of what I've learned and created over these past nine years. I hope that you as coaches, players, and parents will enjoy and benefit from these games and insights.

Acknowledgments

My wife Sally has endured my tennis pursuits—playing, coaching, and now writing—with good humor and cheer, and I thank her for that. I also want to thank her for introducing our three children to tennis at a young age and for encouraging them to pursue the sport. Our now-adult children (Nina, Chelsey, and Tim) deserve effusive thanks for allowing me to participate in some of their early tennis lessons, so I could be involved in their tennis life other than driving and paying fees. I thank Chelsey and Tim for accepting me as an assistant coach during several of their seasons of high school tennis.

Special thanks to Coaches Pete Christofferson and Mark Happel of Verona Area High School and Ben Conklin of Oregon High School for their willingness to accept me as a volunteer assistant coach and for having the trust to allow me to try out, modify, and use my unique training games during practices.

I have learned a tremendous amount from the many Verona Area and Oregon high school players I have had the privilege to train during practices and to observe and coach during matches. I thank all of you for the associations. You have been test cases, at times, when I have experimented with new and revised games, and I hope you have benefited from the experiences. The youngsters and adults to whom I have given private lessons over the years have also been test cases at times, and I thank you for your involvement.

Acknowledgments

Thanks to John Woods, CWL Publishing Enterprises, my book producer, and his associates for doing the detailed and professional work required to turn the manuscript into a book ready for publication. Many thanks go to friends and relatives who provided helpful comments and suggestions as the book progressed. In addition, thanks to my trout fishing friend and professional photographer, Jeremy Jones, for shooting the photos.

About the Author

Terry Geurkink is a board-certified emergency medicine physician, with a career of 25 years of emergency medicine work at St. Marys Hospital Medical Center in Madison, Wisconsin. He is currently semi-retired, doing occasional one- to two-week stints of emergency medical work at Indian Health Service Hospital emergency departments at various sites in the United States. His wife Sally tolerates (usually) his immersion in tennis, and his three children, who all played high school tennis, will occasionally hit tennis balls on the same court as their dad. He has been a volunteer assistant coach with the Verona Area High School girls and boys tennis teams for eight years and also coached with the Oregon High School boys team for one year. Terry (a 5.0 player trapped in a 4.0 body) plays 4.0 USTA league tennis with moderate success, and gives individual and group lessons. He and his wife reside in south-central Wisconsin.

1 Unique Games and Fresh Insights

This book is a valuable resource for middle school and high school tennis coaches. It is a concise resource for tennis players of all ages, from the excited, energetic pre-teens and teens, to the still-ambitious, if slightly creaky oldsters, and all those in between. It is also a fine resource for tennis parents who want to acquire either basic tennis knowledge or intermediate to advanced tennis knowledge. This book is perfectly suited for parents who seek some advice and guidance while they help their children begin the tennis journey and subsequently help them to pursue tennis excellence.

As a coach or player or tennis parent, you will find chapters that are truly helpful to you, that will give you fresh insights into the fascinating game of tennis.

As a coach or player, you will have the opportunity to use some or all of the cooperative and competitive games described in these chapters. You might create a variation of one of these games that you find works better for your training sessions, or perhaps you will create your own game or games that will work best for you.

We know that middle school and high school tennis coaches put in tremendous amounts of time and energy to train their tennis players to be competitive and successful during match play. We also know that every coach needs a variety of approaches to build skills during practice sessions, to help their tennis athletes progress during the season and from season to season.

This book will be valuable to the ambitious coach, because it provides a host of competitive and cooperative small-segment training games. These games cover nearly every aspect of tennis and can be suitably adapted for novice, intermediate, and advanced players. In addition, the book addresses significant items, including basic shot technical training, specialty shot technical training, training for strength and conditioning, and injury prevention.

Each chapter explores key issues and parts of play that every coach should be aware of and knowledgeable about. Coaches who carefully read and digest this book will have the opportunity to upgrade their coaching and training methods.

As a long-time high school tennis team assistant coach, with both boys and girls teams, I have watched many players with specific weaknesses and problem areas in their tennis game. After many hours of thought and then on-court trial and error, I created effective games to address those weaknesses and problems.

I created and fine-tuned these training games to help our athletes improve as fast as possible, as efficiently as possible, and as much as possible. I also created cooperative and competitive games that are fun, efficient, and unique. These games are suitable for high school and middle school players and for adult players of all ages.

In my coaching career, I have trained many boys and girls who have won conference championships, sectional championships, and state tournament matches, and some of these players have gone on to be successful Division 3 college players. Our teams have won conference and sectional championships.

I emphasize my teaching and coaching philosophies, and there is one recurring theme: Teach players the correct techniques and tactics, then place them into carefully structured, small-segment cooperative and competitive training games during practice sessions so they can develop each aspect of the array of tennis skills, using their own athletic gifts.

As coaches, we fantasize about our players taking the court for a big match and boldly using all the techniques and tactics that we have taught them during practice sessions. The reality is starkly different. Most players will eventually master a technique or tactic in practice, but it may be weeks, months, or years before we see them use this skill in a match, and this lag time is a major coaching frustration.

If we place our players into structured competitive games in practice where there is a minor reward for winning and a minor penalty for losing, and the players have the opportunity to hit a huge number of repetitions (reps) under pressure, the learned skill, in my experience, will appear in match play much sooner than would otherwise occur.

This book will definitely be useful for tennis players, from those in middle school to aging adults. For the ambitious players who are motivated to improve, the book's contents give access to unique and competitive games and training techniques that offer a path to playing at a higher level.

Most players, especially experienced adults, prefer to play matches rather than spend time doing "boring drills." However, it is valuable for players of all ages to work on small segments of the whole game. By using well-designed competitive games to do this, players can enjoy the fun of competition and benefit from many reps in specific segments so their skills advance.

I created these games and have played them myself with our high school players and with adult friends. Subsequently I revised them to be maximally useful and efficient. Most of the games concentrate on one skill or one segment of play to isolate parts of the entire game. If players learn, develop, and eventually master each segment, over time they will be able to use these multiple segments to showcase their "whole" game.

As you go through the book you will find specific notes for coaches. These are boxed and headlined **Coaching Tips.** These tips are gleaned from my experiences and observations. These are followed by advice for players. These notes are boxed and headlined **Players' Tips.**

Tennis Parent Perspectives

Tennis parents have major roles to play in assisting their child's quest to learn and master the game. These include:

1. Arranging or helping to arrange their child's participation in lessons, clinics, practices, informal hitting sessions with friends, formal matches, and tournaments.

2. Providing transportation to most or all of the activities noted in "1" above.

3. Footing the bill for racquets, balls, tennis clothing, shoes, lesson fees, clinic fees, camp fees, tournament fees, etc.

4. Supporting their child's involvement in the sport by attending as many of the above activities as possible.

This book gives tennis parents a view of the many components involved in their child's journey to becoming an accomplished player. The book helps parents become more knowledgeable about the game and enhances their enjoyment of watching their child compete. There are many comments regarding the parents' role in relation to their child's tennis development and performance.

Specific notes for parents are boxed and headlined **Parents' Tips.**

In addition, Chapter 19 is specifically written for tennis parents, including the nonplaying, the casual-playing, and the avid/advanced–playing tennis parents.

Consider These Thoughts

In my primary vocation as a long-time emergency medicine physician, I constantly seek methods to treat patients more effectively and more efficiently, especially when work is extremely busy. There are a number of segments involved in taking care of each emergency patient, and many emergency staff members are involved in those segments. One key to efficient emergency medical care is proper sequencing of the diagnostic and treatment segments so the entire process flows smoothly. There is a parallel from this to teaching tennis. The proper sequence of teaching the segments of each shot, each technique, and each tactic is important. I discuss and explain my rationale for certain aspects of sequencing in the book.

As an emergency medicine physician, I have taught hundreds of EMTs, medical students, and resident physicians. Typically, that teaching is done in a pressurized, chaotic, unpredictable environment where any type of patient with any type of life-threatening problem may arrive at any minute. As a welcome contrast—truly a luxury—teaching students on a tennis court can be planned, structured, and calm, without interruptions or emergencies. At the end of a practice or lesson, everyone can leave the court reasonably happy and satisfied, which is often not the case with emergency medicine patient care.

This book is targeted to coaches who work with the novice, intermediate, and advanced players (these three groups comprise 98 percent of the tennis player universe). Elite-level coaches and players (perhaps 2 percent of the tennis universe) should find selected items of interest. In my experience, elite players can definitely benefit from many of the competitive 1 versus 1 games. Tennis parents, with children who are at the novice to elite levels, should also find topics of interest.

2 Live Ball vs. Dead Ball Training and Games

Live ball versus dead ball training is a significant topic in coaching tennis. When coaches decide how to design a practice session and allocate precious practice time, it is helpful to have a clear understanding of the difference between *dead ball* training (where balls are fed to a player by a coach or machine) and *live ball* training (where every ball is hit by a cooperating or competing player).

I am a firm believer that dead ball training has a limited role in teaching tennis, and that role consists of the time spent teaching a new stroke or a stroke variation to players. It works well for the coach to hand toss balls to players when helping them learn the correct stroke mechanics. In these close quarters, it is fairly easy for the coach to observe exactly what the players are doing, both right and wrong. The coach can repeatedly demonstrate the correct mechanics and can have the players repeatedly shadow drill the correct mechanics.

Particularly for novice players, the hand-tossed ball is unintimidating compared to balls coming off the racquet from a distance or from the other side of the net.

When players have learned the basic mechanics of a stroke, I believe it is important for them to advance to either cooperative or competitive live ball games as the next stage of learning, typically using a mini-tennis format.

Live ball games have clear-cut advantages. During these games, the player must:

1. Closely observe the opponent to see their body position and their racquet motion, and then anticipate the type of ball that will be coming off the opponent's racquet. (Note: This anticipation skill—a combination of visual inputs and brain processing—is a subtle, but important one that typically can only be learned and honed by thousands of reps of observation. A player can't learn this by hitting balls coming out of a ball machine or by hitting balls served by a coach.)

2. Closely observe the ball coming off the opponent's racquet and make split-second judgments (again, a combination of visual inputs and brain processing) as to the flight path, pace, and spin of the ball, and then start to move to the optimal position to return the ball. (Note: This collection of skills must be learned and honed by thousands of reps. Seeing balls coming out of machines or off a coach's racquet does not teach this.)

3. Use optimal footwork to get into the best setup position to hit the ball. Given the unpredictable nature of balls coming off the opponent's racquet, compared to the relatively predictable nature of balls coming out of the ball machine or off the coach's racquet, the footwork required is more intense and demanding. It takes thousands of reps to learn the optimal footwork to attain the optimal setup position for hitting a quality return shot.

4. Hit the ball to the opponent's side of the court with intent to hit it at the opponent or away from the opponent to one side or the other, with a certain flight path, pace, and spin. These are intricate, split-second judgments that require thousands of reps to train the brain and muscles to perform these tasks at a high level. They cannot be duplicated by hitting against a stationary, inanimate ball machine or a nearly immobile feeding coach.

The player must learn how various opponents will react to various shots. Can the opponent effectively reach and return a topspin drive to the forehand or backhand corner? Can the opponent get to and return an excellent drop shot or a mediocre drop shot or a poor drop shot? Can the opponent hit a clear winner off a midcourt sitter? Can the opponent backpedal and hit a topspin lob for an overhead winner?

Every player must make hundreds of decisions regarding shot selections in a single match. Each player needs thousands of competitive reps in training sessions to learn which shots will be most successful against certain types of players, so the player can make high-percentage shot selection decisions during match play.

In summary, the coach should use hand-fed balls to teach stroke mechanics only. All other court practice time should be spent doing live ball competitive games and live ball cooperative games (see Chapter 7).

Coaching Tips

Set aside time during practice sessions to teach and re-teach stroke techniques. If your athletes learn and maintain good technical skills, they will have the opportunity to use their athletic talents to continuously improve. If, however, their technical skills are poor, they will have great difficulty progressing along the desired performance curve.

If your players do a few reps with correct technique, they will benefit far more than if they do hundreds of reps using an incorrect technique.

It takes a huge effort on the coach's part to closely observe each player's technical skills and then to correct the items that need correcting. However, there is a payoff in terms of raising the ceiling on the player's ultimate level of performance.

Several years ago when working with a standout senior doubles player who was struggling with her forehand topspin ground strokes, I realized she was using the continental grip to hit these shots. It was unclear how long she had been doing this, perhaps a few months, but perhaps her whole high school career. It was not a surprise that she was struggling with this shot, since it is almost impossible to hit a quality topspin forehand using the continental grip. We did some intense training on grip re-modeling, which helped her with this shot for the rest of the season.

Players' Tips

Friends can often teach each other proper technique, and trade knowledge gleaned from other sources. Using some hand-tossed balls for teaching a specific stroke and then a selection of proper competitive or cooperative games to compile repetitions, players can act as the teaching pro for each other.

Parents' Tips

You have a vested interest in what your child is learning during lessons, clinics, camps, and team practices. It is reasonable for you to ask the coach about the level of emphasis on teaching correct fundamental skills.

I have worked with many high school players who have had extensive tennis training with teaching "pros" via private lessons and camps, and some of these players have unproductive techniques and habits. I believe a conscientious instructor should have corrected these items during prior training. It takes concentrated effort on the instructor's part to closely examine what players are doing. Then that instructor must use every means possible to teach the correct fundamentals and help players embed these fundamentals so players have the opportunity to reach their true potential.

3 Competitive Training Games 1:
Maximizing Touches per Practice Hour

Consider these points:

1. Each time a player contacts a ball in a practice session, the player learns and records small fragments of skill and knowledge, either consciously or unconsciously. The visual system, brain, and muscles combine to allow the player to anticipate the ball's flight path, pace, and spin as it leaves the opponent's racquet, process and react to the cues perceived from the incoming ball, and set up to return the ball with a specific flight path, pace, and spin.

2. Each time a player contacts a ball in a practice session and succeeds in achieving the objective in a competitive game, the player learns and records small fragments of skill and knowledge.

3. Each time a player contacts a ball in a practice session and fails to achieve the objective in a competitive game, the player learns and records small fragments of skill and knowledge. It may be true that the record of this failure is imprinted more heavily than the information recorded after a success.

Consider these scenarios:

Scenario 1: 4 players are on a court with 1 coach. To practice a particular stroke, they take turns hitting a fed ball from the coach. Each player might average 4 touches per minute. In a 1-hour practice session of this type, each player would hit 240 balls. If there are 30 similar practices in a season, each player would hit 7,200 balls.

Scenario 2: 4 players are on a court playing a 2 v 2 competitive mini-tennis game or a competitive full-court game. Each player might average 10 touches per minute, compared to 4 per minute in scenario 1, a ratio of 2.5 to 1. In a 1-hour practice session of this type, each player would hit 600 balls. If there are 30 similar practices in a season, each player would hit 18,000 balls.

Scenario 3: 4 players are on a court playing 2 simultaneous 1 v 1 competitive mini-tennis games or partial court–width baseline games. Each player might average 20 touches per minute, compared to 4 per minute in scenario 1, a ratio of 5 to 1. In a 1-hour practice session of this type, each player would hit 1,200 balls. If there are 30 similar practices in a season, each player would hit 36,000 balls.

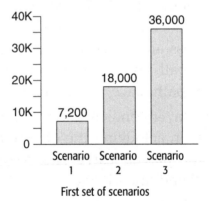

First set of scenarios

Now consider these additional scenarios:

A high school coach has 12 players to supervise and train and has the use of 2 courts and 60 minutes of direct court time. This coach has to make choices as to how to allocate the court time and practice time. The choices could look like this:

Scenario 1: 4 players play a doubles challenge match on court

#1, lasting 60 minutes, and each player averages 2 touches per minute, and 120 touches in the 60 minutes. The coach works with the other 8 players during this time on court #2, feeding balls in rotating order to each of the 8 players as they work on stroke development. Each player averages 2 touches per minute and totals 120 touches in 60 minutes. If there are 30 similar practices in a season, each player would hit 3,600 balls.

Scenario 2: 4 players are playing 2 separate 1 v 1 competitive mini-tennis games, or 1 v 1 baseline partial-width games simultaneously on court #1, and they average 20 touches per minute each. Every 20 minutes, a new group of 4 players rotates to this court. Each player averages 400 touches during their allotted 20 minutes on this court. At the same time, on court #2, the coach feeds balls to 8 players as they work on stroke development. Each player spends a total of 40 minutes on this court and averages 2 touches per minute, for a total of 80 touches. In this scenario, at the end of a 60-minute practice, each player will total 480 touches. If there are 30 similar practices in a season, each player would hit 14,400 balls.

Scenario 3: The coach spends the first 10 minutes of practice time teaching a selected stroke. During this time, each of the 12 players does 10 shadow drill strokes, and each player hits 4 hand-tossed balls. For the next 50 minutes, 6 players are assigned to each of the 2 courts. On each court, 4 players play 2 separate 1 v 1 competitive mini-tennis games, or 1 v 1 baseline partial-width games simultaneously. Every 2 minutes, the coach has the players rotate one spot, so the 2 players sitting out will then rotate onto the court. During the 50 minutes, each player will be on the court competing for about 32 minutes. At an average of 20 touches per minute, each player would total 640 touches. If there are 30 similar practices in a season, each player would hit 19,200 balls.

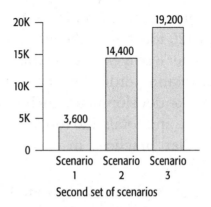

Second set of scenarios

Coaching Tips

The raw numbers tell a powerful story. Each touch helps the player accumulate fragments of skill and knowledge. The quantity of touches per hour of practice time is vital, assuming the touches are done correctly. It is essential to set up practice scenarios in which players are taught the correct mechanics, techniques, and tactics, and then are given court time to practice those ingredients, with opportunities to accumulate a huge number of cooperative and competitive touches per practice session.

Players' Tips

If you are willing to discipline yourself to use correct mechanics, techniques, and tactics and to commit to a significant amount of court time doing competitive training games, your level of play will improve automatically, which is a wonderful byproduct of your effort and time.

Parents' Tips

If your child participates in group lessons, and you note that your child spends a significant portion of the session standing in line waiting for a turn to hit a ball, consider politely asking the instructor about his or her philosophy of tennis instruction. If the instructor is unaware of the importance of touches per practice session, this should prompt you to be concerned about the quality of instruction your child is receiving.

4 Competitive Training Games 2: Motivating Our Players

As coaches, we seek to conduct practices that are efficient, productive, and fulfilling for our players and ourselves. We want to motivate our players so they seek to improve every time they step on the court for a practice session.

We recognize that some of our players are highly motivated and show up for practice with energy, resolve, and focus, and simply need structure and teaching to develop. Other players arrive at practice with less energy, less resolve, less focus, and less motivation. We need to be creative and clever in structuring training sessions to get these players revved up to focus and work at a high level.

Competitive training games, with consequences for winners and losers, can provide motivation for players to perform in practice. If players get a high number of repetitions of basic and advanced shots and a high number of repetitions while competing in multiple situations, their match play will invariably improve.

My experience has taught me that we don't have to conduct magical practices for our players to improve, but we do have to provide the proper framework for our ambitious players to seize the opportunity to advance their skills. We also must give our less ambitious players the opportunity to improve, with the possibility that at some point in their high school careers (or perhaps in post–high school play), this group of players will catch fire, and their ambitions will soar.

We can instruct our players on tactics and strategies, but most players learn these lessons best by competing in small-segment games in which they experience success or failure, depending partly on the tactics they use. If they fail, they receive a direct incentive to change or improve their tactical decisions. When our players lose a competitive training game to a teammate, this should motivate the loser to scrutinize the tactics their winning opponent used and mimic them. A training game loss can provide the coach with a suitable "teachable moment" to review a tactic and the rationale behind it.

In the chapters to follow, I list and describe many competitive training games, covering nearly every facet of tennis play. These games provide structure, repetitions, and incentives to players to perform at a high level and to hit the ball with precision during practice sessions. As a result, the players and coaches can exit a practice session with a solid sense of accomplishment and productivity.

Players need to be challenged to compete in training games, and the challenges need to fit their level of skill. Novice players need competitive games that are structured so they can get in a high number of reps with a low level of difficulty. Likewise, intermediate players need to compete at a moderate level of difficulty, and the advanced players need to compete in a structure that provides a high level of difficulty. This book provides coaching tips that help you structure these competitive games to fit your players so they can train at a level commensurate with their skills.

I also provide tips for players of all ages so as you use these tightly structured games, you receive insight into how the games will help you improve your play and performance.

Rewards for players for winning these competitive games can be, for example, the opportunity to hold their racquet high to signify they are winners, the opportunity to rest while their losing opponent does a required exercise, the opportunity to watch while the loser picks up tennis balls, some extra verbal praise from the coach for competing hard and winning, etc.

Consequences of losing these competitive games can be, for example, a required exercise that is quick, but beneficial, such as 2–5 pushups, a quick sprint around the net, core exercises that the coach teaches and then labels with a number (I currently use 5 core exercises), split-steps and shadow strokes from the baseline to the net, picking up the balls, etc.

The coach should tailor the consequences to fit the players he or she is working with. For boys, jumping jacks may be scorned, and for girls, multiple push-ups may be too onerous. Some days, the consequences for losing could be a bit wacky: for girls, losers could be required to sing and/or dance for 10 seconds. (I have used this frequently, and the girls love it.) For boys, winners could pick the exercise that the losers do, or winners could pick the next competitive game to play. Use creativity to keep players guessing what the rewards and consequences will be, and consistently try to motivate your players to compete at a high level in these training games.

Coaching Tips

As you learn through trial and error what motivates your players to practice at a high level of focus and intensity, refine your rewards and penalties as the season progresses. This is one of the fun and creative parts of coaching that, if done successfully, is definitely satisfying.

You might consider a radically different approach to motivating your players, which can be effective with selected players and teams. At the conclusion of a competitive training game or practice set, the winner is required to tell the loser what made the winner successful. These key factors might include one or more of the following: footwork, consistency, precision, focus, effort, desire to win, shot selection, shot execution, techniques, and tactics. This communication from the winner to his or her losing teammate could be a top-notch motivator, teaching tool, and feedback mechanism for the loser. The reverse approach can also be used, in which case the loser is required to tell the winner the factors that led to the loss.

When we use these two methods, our players gain better insight into their strengths and weaknesses, and they enhance their ability to do self-coaching during matches. By doing self-critiques with a teammate, our players do peer-to-peer coaching that we, as adult coaches, cannot duplicate. The communication required by these methods can be a major challenge for our quiet and shy players, but one of our roles as coaches is to challenge our players to move beyond their comfort zone.

Players' Tips

You may not need a reward or penalty to be motivated in these competitive games because the desire to win each one may be enough in itself to generate high levels of energy and effort. However, you might want to experiment with some self-created rewards and penalties, and see what the results are.

Parents' Tips

You are most often the key to your child's introduction to the game. If your child subsequently is motivated to learn and compete in this wonderful game, your role is to assist him or her in their journey. I suggest that you be aware that your motivation (to be the parent of an active or accomplished tennis player) is not the same as your child's motivation, and that you allow your child the opportunity to ask about expanding their tennis opportunities, rather than steadily arranging opportunities for her or him.

5 Competitive Training Games 3:
Enhancing the Psychological and Emotional Development of Our Players

There is a subtle but important benefit derived from using competitive training games during practice sessions. We know that our players respond to the pressure of matches, especially big matches, in a variety of ways. Some players love to be on the big stage and they perform their best against the top competition. Others struggle with their performance, confidence, and attitude when faced with a key match or a key set or a crucial point.

As coaches, we realize our players who play big in showcase matches have "the right stuff," and we don't need to do a thing to assist their psychological state. They need technical and tactical guidance, but they do not need a pep talk or psychological guidance.

Other players, however, exhibit some difficulties with pressure matches for an almost unlimited number of reasons. The astute coach may have some extraordinary abilities to assist these players before or during matches, using creative approaches. There are many self-help books written for this very purpose, but there may be a simpler, better way to assist these players: putting them under pressure every day in practice, in small doses, using structured competitive training games. These training games help them learn to cope with pressure, disappointment, success, and failure, which occur on a daily basis, rather than only on match days.

Consider this breakdown of a practice session lasting 1.75 hours:

1. Warm-up drills, balance drills, stretching: 10 minutes.
2. Fluid breaks and downtime between segments: 15 minutes.
3. Technical instruction and cooperative games to enhance technical learning: 20 minutes.
4. Competitive training games: 60 minutes.

During the 60 minutes of competitive training games, each player might engage in 5–15 separate small-segment games. Each player typically competes against teammates of similar skill levels, and each game features a reward and/or penalty at its conclusion.

Each player in each game understands the rules of the competition, develops judgments regarding his or her competitor(s) in the game, and engages in the competition with a certain level of physical, mental, and psychological commitment. Each player makes subtle adjustments during the game, depending on how he or she is playing, and how his or her opponent(s) are playing. If the player is committed to winning, he or she will focus and compete to the maximum, and will know the result in 2–10 minutes, depending on the game, and the coach's decision regarding the length of the contest.

The time required for this whole process to occur is relatively short, but it contains all the physical, mental, and psychological components of a 3-hour, 3-set match for the conference championship, although surely without the same levels of intensity.

It is reasonable to believe that by putting players into small-segment competitive training games frequently, they develop some or many of the traits we look for in our successful athletes: focus on the task at hand, full engagement in the competition, confidence, calmness, the ability to adjust as the contest progresses, and the ability to play well at the end of a close contest.

Instead of having your players drill for the 60 minutes of practice time (not at all comparable to a competitive game or match) or having them play a "practice set" for the 60 minutes of practice time (one prolonged segment of competition), use multiple small-segment competitive training games during this 60 minutes and realize that your players are going through a vital maturation process in a structured, efficient manner.

Coaching Tips

Few coaches are MS or PhD sports psychologists, but most are amateur sports psychologists. Using the above approach to "psychological training," we may do our players a great service by allowing them the opportunities to develop their own "on-court" psychological skills and maturity. In addition, when players exhibit emotional or psychological immaturity during these competitive training games (throwing racquets, cursing, giving the game away with out-of-control shots), it provides the perfect teaching moment for the coach, in the practice setting, which is a better time to intervene than during a key match.

A few years ago, one of our best doubles players "froze" in a state tournament match. It appeared to be a case of "stage fright" and, unfortunately, it lasted the entire match, which led to an unhappy result. In retrospect, if this player had done hundreds of small-segment competitive training games during practices, the player might have handled this situation better.

Players' Tips

Few of us perform regularly to our maximum potential in match play, especially important matches. If we put in some practice time doing these small-segment competitive training games, and perhaps take 1–2 minutes at the conclusion of each one to discuss our performance with our training partner, we may do some positive self-help psychological work without hiring a sports psychologist or reading expensive self-help books.

In the past year, I was doing a few small-segment competitive training games with some tennis league teammates. After the first 2 minutes of one game, one of the players refused to play anymore, saying the game was "too difficult" for him. Did he learn anything from this? I'm not sure, but we learned that he could not psychologically handle doing poorly in this setting. I also realized that some players are more comfortable doing cooperative games, at least until their skill levels are adequate to enter into competitive games.

Parents' Tips

The arena of psychological and emotional performance by your tennis child is one you should avoid entering, unless you are careful and tactful.

In the past I have watched some players in junior tournaments (no coach is involved) act with immaturity, including bashing balls out of the court after losing a point, yelling at opponents, throwing their racquets, etc. You as a tennis parent could make a smart decision in this case: Ask a tournament official to stop the match due to your child's immature behavior and forfeit games or the match. Follow this action by not allowing your child to play another match for some specified period. Preventing your child from playing matches and allowing him or her to think about the immature behavior for weeks or months may be a powerful motivator for a change in behavior.

I've witnessed a few tennis parents berate their child after he or she lost a match, and it is not a pretty sight. It is far better for parents to allow their child significant time to process a loss, and to avoid "coaching" them after a loss.

Kids learn a ton all by themselves while losing a match, and if there is teaching to be done, it is best done by your child's coach or instructor or your child's friends.

Support your child's performance honestly but briefly, whether they win or lose, such as: after a loss, "Tough loss" or "Great effort"; and after a win, "Nice match" or "Great play." Most kids hate to be harangued after a loss, and hate to be slobbered on after a win.

6 Competitive Training Games 4: Development of Our Novice Players

Some high school coaches have the luxury of greeting incoming freshman players who have had years of tennis training, extensive experience in tournament competition, and tournament success, and who are polished and elite players.

These players may have averaged a 1-hour lesson per week for 6 years, or about 300 hours of training. They may have played 5 tournaments per year for 6 years, including an average of 3 matches per tournament, at an average of 1.5 hours per match: a total of 135 hours of competitive match play. The coaching challenge with these rare players is to keep them interested in improvement during their high school careers and to successfully guide their continued development.

Most high school coaches welcome incoming freshman players who have varying degrees of athletic talent and either zero or minimal previous tennis training. Some freshmen are self-taught to a degree and carry the baggage of ingrained bad habits. These players typically have never played a formal match or participated in a tournament. These players are developmental projects. Some will develop a true passion for the game and within 1, 2, or 3 years, they will be highly competitive varsity players.

Some will play JV tennis for 1–4 years, and enjoy the experience, but not have the desire or drive or talent to play at a higher level.

I have worked with several players who as freshmen were the rawest of novice tennis players, without notable athletic talents, and who appeared to be destined for a career as mediocre JV players. But at some point during their high school careers, they "caught fire" and developed a burning desire to achieve and a terrific work ethic to accompany that desire. At the point when these players caught fire, their skills and level of play advanced at an incredible rate, and they became solid and sometimes outstanding varsity players.

Coaches using well-structured practice sessions, including technical instruction, cooperative training games, and competitive training games, can assist these highly motivated players to realize their dreams and their potential.

The typical novice player, with moderate athletic talent and ambitions to be a top player, gains significant benefits from the opportunity to compete in small-segment competitive and cooperative training games during every practice session.

If we offer these novice players some basic technical training and then place them into structured small-segment training games in every practice session, they may find that they have some natural talent in one or more segments. If they start to have some success in even one segment of play (for example, playing mini-tennis using forehand topspin shots only), this may provide a key building block for them to find success in other segments.

If the novice player fails occasionally or fails often during small-segment competitive training games and does three pushups after every loss, the feedback cycle will be intact and simple: Lose the 2–3-minute game, and there is an immediate experience of short-term failure with a small amount of pain. However, if the novice wins the 2–3-minute game, there is an immediate experience of short-term exhilaration and accomplishment. The novice player has an opportunity to learn something from each loss and each win.

I think it is illuminating to examine some of the actual hours compiled by the novice player versus the experienced player year by year.

Freshman Season: Before the First Practice

Experienced Player: 300 hours of training and 135 hours of match play.

Novice: 0 hours of training and 0 hours of match play.

During the season, both attend 30 practice sessions of 1.75 hours each, so total practice time equals 52.5 hours. The novice learns the technical aspects of the basic strokes (forehand and backhand topspin, forehand and backhand volleys, serve) and competes in 12 JV matches, each lasting 45 minutes on average, for a total match time of 9 hours. The experienced player refines technical and tactical aspects of play and competes in 30 varsity matches, each lasting 1.5 hours on average, for a total of 45 hours.

During each of the 30 practice sessions, they both do 20 minutes of technical training and cooperative games, for a total of 10 hours.

During each of the 30 practice sessions, they both do 60 minutes of competitive games (this time could include standard singles or doubles match play), for a total of 30 hours.

Freshman Season After the Last Practice

Experienced Player: 310 hours of training and 210 hours of match play and competitive games.

Novice: 10 hours of training and 39 hours of match play and competitive games.

Off-Season Between Freshman and Sophomore Years

Both players may or may not seek training and competition to enhance their skills.

Sophomore Season

Assume the same numbers for both players as during the freshman season. The novice player improves on the technical aspects of the basic strokes (forehand and backhand topspin, forehand and backhand volleys, serve) and learns the forehand and backhand slice shots. The experienced player continues to hone a wide array of shots, and works on tactical training.

Sophomore Season After the Last Practice

Experienced Player: 320 hours of training and 285 hours of match play and competitive games.

Novice: 20 hours of training and 78 hours of match play and competitive games.

Off-Season Between Sophomore and Junior Years

Both players may or may not seek training and competition to enhance their skills.

Junior Season

Assume both players have the same practice numbers as the first two seasons and they work on enhancing their technical and tactical skills and that now both players play 30 varsity matches.

Junior Season After the Last Practice

Experienced Player: 330 hours of training and 360 hours of match play and competitive games

Novice: 30 hours of training and 153 hours of match play and competitive games

Coaching Tips

One fact is crystal clear: The huge gap between the experienced player and the novice at the start of their freshman year can be narrowed somewhat, but will never close unless the novice embarks on a highly ambitious off-season regimen that includes high hours of training and match play. However, by providing the novice with at least an hour per practice session of competitive training games, I believe we give this category of player the best opportunity to reach their playing potential as they progress through their high school career.

Players' Tips

If you are ambitious and start your career as a novice freshman player, you have the opportunity to develop over your high school career and, perhaps, become a fine player as a junior or senior, possibly even as a sophomore. For this to happen you must be committed to putting in time to learn the technical skills and to compete in match play and competitive training games.

Several years ago, our team had a freshman player who played at the #5 JV doubles level her freshman year. She was ambitious, wanted to learn, and was open-minded about accepting advice, meaning she was coachable. She sought extra help after practices and during optional late-season practices. She put in training time during the off-season and arrived at tryouts for her sophomore season ready to compete. A large number of seniors had graduated, and we had many girls competing for open varsity spots. After several weeks of tryouts, practices, and matches, this girl became a fixture at #1 varsity doubles. She took the extraordinary jump of eight levels of play from her freshman year to her sophomore year.

For adult players who want to improve or move up a rating level, you must find a way to obtain technical training and spend time doing competitive training games as well as play matches. The combination of these three endeavors will almost surely give you the satisfaction of playing at a higher level.

Parents' Tips

This chapter gives you an idea how the hours of technical training, cooperative training games, competitive training games, and match play add up over several years.

There is no mystery to these facts: Athletically talented young kids who love tennis and put in hours learning and playing the game will have advanced skills and are likely to be successful when they start playing high school tennis. Athletically talented kids who love the game but who are just learning and playing tennis as high school freshmen will have limited skills and success until they have dedicated significant hours learning both fundamentals and advanced skills and competing in training games and matches.

Parents, it's crucial that you practice patience as your child develops her or his tennis and athletic skills. Keep in mind that kids develop at different ages and different rates. I have watched junior players over time who, at ages 12 and 13, were physically less developed than their peers and who could not win a match in junior tournaments, but who gradually developed strength, speed, and coordination and became outstanding high school players.

7 Cooperative Training Games

ooperative training games are defined by a situation where a player's goal is to do what is required to assist fellow players to develop or improve a stroke or skill or tactic. There are times when cooperative games are efficient learning tools. In a friendly rather than an adversarial game, the emphasis is to help your teammate rather than defeat your teammate.

There are many cooperative games, some of which I detail in upcoming chapters, and they are one more approach to assisting your players along the tennis learning curve.

Coaching Tips

As I point out when going through the steps to teach certain technical skills, cooperative games are a transition from direct instruction by the coach to competitive games with other players.

Use cooperative games as a change of pace during a practice session. For example, a 1.75-hour practice session could consist of:

1. 10 minutes for warm-ups, balance drill, and stretching.

2. Small-segment competitive games for 30 minutes.

3. 5-minute fluid and rest break.

4. The coach teaches a technical skill over a 15-minute period.

5. The newly taught technical skill is used in a cooperative game for 10 minutes.

6. 5-minute fluid and rest break.

7. 30 minutes of small-segment competitive games.

In my experience, girls particularly enjoy cooperative games, and boys tend to be less than fond of them. Cooperative games present an opportunity for the coach to participate in the game, closely observe what each player is doing, and then do instruction and corrective coaching as needed.

Players' Tips

This is an excellent way for friends to help each other learn and improve certain strokes and shots without the need to hire a teaching pro.

Parents' Tips

If you are a casual or avid player, you may have a better experience with your child playing cooperative games rather than competitive games. Experiment with both, but if you note that you or your child seems unhappy, angry, or frustrated during competitive games, consider limiting your on-court play to cooperative games.

8 Before the Games Begin

Warm-Ups

Team warm-ups are an important first element in practice sessions, because they set the tone for the entire practice. The warm-up session should be brief, perhaps 3–5 minutes, high-paced, and productive.

An example for girls and boys: The team lines up on the baseline of one or two courts and does a series of footwork drills with racquets in hand, going up to the net and returning to the baseline.

An example for girls and boys: A split-step/power skip drill in which each player split-steps at every line intersection on a court, moving right to left, in a designated pattern, and then power skips to the third court over, does a split-step pattern on that court from left to right, and power skips back to the first court.

An example for girls: The "team amoeba warm-up," in which the team joins hands to form a closed chain. The players must keep the circle intact while doing a series of maneuvers around the courts at a fast pace. This provides a good warm-up and team-building exercise at the same time.

An example for boys: All start at the baseline, do several shadow strokes, then drop and do five pushups, do more shadow strokes, then drop and do a specified core exercise, etc.

Balance Drills

Balance drills are an efficient way to improve proprioception (feedback from muscles and nerves regarding position in space) and to help prevent knee and ankle injuries. They can be simple and fun.

For example, everyone balances on their left foot while doing a forehand volley shadow drill for 30 seconds with eyes open, then 30 seconds with the eyes closed. Then, balance on the right foot while doing shadow backhand volleys, 30 seconds with the eyes open, then 30 seconds with the eyes closed. Pick variations to do during the balance drills and keep the enthusiasm high, because preventing significant knee injuries (such as the dreaded ACL—anterior cruciate ligament—tears), second- and third-degree ankle sprains, and other ankle injuries is crucial. Any of these injuries result in most or all of the season lost to injury.

Stretching

Some type of stretching is a positive activity, although the true physiologic benefits are debated, and the timing, whether before practice or after practice, is contested.

I promote the "1-minute tennis stretch," which is simple, fairly complete, and fast. Each player finds a spot on the outer fence and starts with a "wall lean," alternating feet forward, then a quad stretch by using ankle lifts, followed by trunk stretches, and finally, shoulder rotations both ways.

Coaching Tips

This is a good time to use creativity, devise various warm-ups, balance, and stretching activities. Keep your athletes guessing as to what will happen at the start of each practice.

Players' Tips

You are on your own. There is no coach to demand certain warm-up, balance, or stretching activities. So be smart, and be the type of player to put in several minutes doing some or all of these activities before you start hitting tennis balls.

9 Technical Training for Common Shots

This chapter contains detailed ideas for teaching technical skills, primarily for novice and intermediate players, but also for advanced players who have deficiencies in selected areas. I have included this information because I think it has significant value for coaches and players, with emphasis on some key points. Currently there are a number of books that concentrate on the technical aspects of tennis, but I believe this chapter is a succinct and handy reference for coaches and players.

Two ingredients must be combined to produce a successful tennis player. If a player has tremendous competitive drive and athletic skills and gives great effort on every ball, point, game, set, and match, but lacks a mastery of basic and advanced shots, the player will have a difficult time succeeding. If a player has mastery of all the basic, advanced, and specialty shots, but lacks a high-level competitive drive or athleticism and does not give consistent, great effort, this player will not be successful either. But a player who combines shot mastery with a strong competitive drive and effort has the keys to success.

Note: All technical instructions in this chapter are for right-handed players; instructions for left-handed players are the mirror images.

Teaching the Correct Grips

Teach the players to know what the second MCP joint (the metacarpal-phalangeal joint) is on their dominant hand, and nondominant hand. It is the large joint or knuckle where the index finger joins the hand, denoted by the black circle in the following four photos.

Teach the players to count the bevels on the racquet handle, in both clockwise and counterclockwise directions. With the racquet held in a vertical position, the top bevel is #1.

The Semi-Western Grip

For the forehand topspin, the second MCP joint of the right hand is on the 4th bevel, counting clockwise.

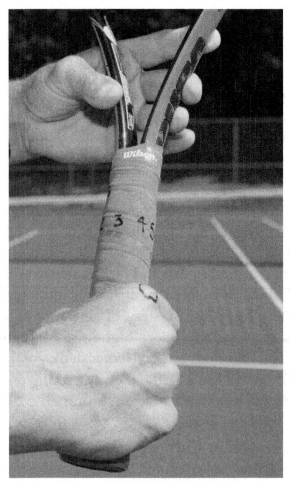

Semi-Western grip

The Continental Grip

For serves, volleys, slices, drop shots, overheads, slice lobs, and defensive slices, the second MCP joint of the right hand is on the 2nd bevel, counting clockwise.

Continental grip

The Two-Hand Backhand Topspin Grip

The left hand has the second MCP joint on the 4th bevel, counting counterclockwise (the left hand Semi-Western forehand topspin grip); the right hand has the second MCP joint on bevel #1.5, counting clockwise. The hands should touch but not overlap. (See photos on page 40.)

Left-hand grip for the two-hand backhand topspin

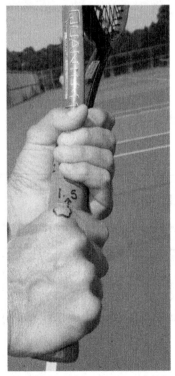

Right-hand grip for the two-hand backhand topspin

The One-Hand Backhand Topspin Grip. The right hand has the second MCP joint on bevel #1.

Coaching Tips

It is a constant challenge to monitor our novice, intermediate, and even advanced players to help them consistently use the correct grips. This part of the technical foundation is important, for without the correct grips, our players may never fulfill their potentials.

Several years ago I had the opportunity to closely observe a terrifically athletic and coordinated tennis player, who played for a nearby school. I watched him over his four-year high school varsity career. As a freshman, he used unorthodox grips, groundstrokes, and volleys. He made them work, and he won the conference #4 varsity singles championship. As a sophomore, he moved up to the #2 varsity singles spot, using the same unorthodox grips and strokes. Due to lack of development, he didn't place in the conference tournament. During his junior and senior seasons, he played #1 singles and, though he was bigger, stronger, faster, and incredibly coordinated, he did not place because his progress had stalled. The unorthodox grips and strokes prevented him from developing the pace and spin he needed to compete successfully at the top level.

If we can teach our novice and intermediate middle schoolers and our high school freshmen the correct grips and stroke mechanics and convince our players to use them consistently, we will likely have the satisfaction of seeing them blossom into good players as their high school careers unfold.

Players' Tips

You must use self-discipline to learn and use the correct grips and stroke mechanics. You can learn them from a knowledgeable friend, a good instructor, or a good YouTube video, but learn them you must if you want to advance your tennis skills and your level of play.

Parents' Tips

The best gift you can give to your tennis-loving child is the opportunity to learn the correct fundamentals, including grips and strokes. If your child learns these crucial building blocks, their desire to play, compete, and improve, and their genetic athletic gifts will be unleashed.

Teaching the Forehand Topspin

I have players start with a short grip, with the index finger through the throat of the racket and the thumb and other fingers on the handle. This gives them maximum racquet control.

There are three basic methods used to hit the forehand topspin shot: the pull-up (or reverse forehand, although I find this to be an awkward name), the classical, and the modern (or windshield wiper).

The finish position using the forehand topspin pull-up method

I teach the pull-up method first, starting with a medium loop and swinging low to high, finishing over the right shoulder. This is an important stroke to learn. It is used by many pro players, such as Nadal, in groundstroke rallies (typically when moving to the forehand side, and when moving to the forehand side and away from the net), and also used for topspin lobs This is the simplest method for virtually all players to learn in order to master hitting the ball with topspin, since the racquet follows a severe low to high path, which is required to brush up on the ball to impart topspin.

I hand toss balls for players to hit after one bounce so I am close to them, and I can carefully observe their footwork and stroke mechanics and give immediate feedback.

The players do reps with this initial grip until they have a smooth stroke and consistently hit the ball with topspin. At that point I have them switch to a short semiwestern grip. As they become proficient with this grip, I have them gradually progress to a full-length semiwestern grip.

The next method I teach is the classical forehand topspin: Start with a medium loop, swing the racquet from low to high, and finish over the left shoulder, while catching the racquet throat with the left hand.

When the players have a smooth classical forehand and produce consistent topspin, I teach them the modern forehand: Start with a medium loop, swing the racquet from low to high, and finish across the left upper arm.

Coaching Tips

In my experience, some novice players can hit quality topspin shots in the first 15 minutes of their first lesson, using the forehand pull-up technique and a short grip. The short grip provides racquet control, which is essential. I find that once the player gets this shot grooved, it is reasonably easy to progress to the classical forehand, and eventually, to the modern forehand.

Players' Tips

If you cannot hit all three varieties of the forehand topspin, consider taking a few lessons so you can get comfortable with at least two of the three methods, with one being the pull-up technique, because it is an excellent shot for several situations, including the topspin lob.

Teaching the 2-Hand Backhand Topspin

1. Have players start with a short grip, with the index finger of the left hand through the throat of the racket, and the thumb and other fingers on the handle. This gives players maximum racquet control.

2. Have the players use a medium-length pendulum backswing, with knees bent, using only the left hand on the racquet. The swing will be from low to high, finishing over the right shoulder, and catching the racquet handle with the right hand.

3. Once players are consistent with this motion doing shadow swings, give them hand-tossed balls to hit after one bounce, until they can hit with a smooth motion and consistent topspin.

4. Next, have the players use a short semiwestern grip with the left hand only on the racquet, and repeat #3.

5. When the players are successful at #4, have them add the right hand primarily as a guide hand. The right-hand second MCP joint is on bevel #1.5, and the hands should touch but not overlap.

Hand toss balls until the players have reasonable success with a smooth motion and hit with consistent topspin.

Coaching Tips

I do not teach novice players the one-hand backhand topspin shot, because it may be the most difficult tennis shot to master, and our novice players will never have the training time to master this during their high school careers. I have seen a number of self-taught players who enter their freshman season using this shot, unsuccessfully for the most part. They are stubborn, refusing to change to the two-hand backhand, and they never develop an adequate backhand topspin shot during their four years of high school competition.

In contrast, the two-hand backhand topspin shot is one of the easiest shots to learn and master. I can typically teach a novice player to hit a quality two-hand backhand topspin shot in 15–20 minutes.

In the past, one of our players started his freshman season with a good forehand topspin, a good serve, a fair backhand slice, and no backhand topspin. He played three years with this combination with only moderate success. However, before his senior season, he finally learned and mastered the two-hand backhand topspin. With nice balance hitting from both sides, he won a conference championship in his final season.

Players' Tips

Make an honest assessment of your time commitment to tennis training and your tennis goals. If you have limited time to commit to training, but want to compete at a fairly high level (as in high school varsity or in a 3.5 or 4.0 league), find a way to learn the two-hand backhand topspin shot. This shot works beautifully during return of serve and ground-stroke rallies, and it will not hinder you from developing an excellent backhand slice or a solid one-hand backhand volley.

Parents' Tips

This is one technical skill that you should pay attention to, as your child is developing his or her tennis fundamentals. If your child is being pushed by an instructor or coach to learn a one-hand backhand topspin shot, I strongly recommend that you discuss this with the instructor or coach, so you understand their rationale for promoting this shot. In addition, you and your child must understand the tremendous amount of training time it will take to master this difficult shot.

Teaching Forehand Volleys

1. I teach the neutral position in this way: Right hand with the continental grip (short to start), left hand with thumb, index finger, and middle finger on the bottom part of the frame. The racquet is exactly vertical and neutral. The top of the racquet is just below the eyes, because it is difficult and unnecessary to track an incoming ball with the racquet in the visual path.

Forehand volley position

2. Players start with a shortened continental grip for all-important racquet control. I have them start by positioning the racquet slightly in front and to the right side. With their wrist locked, the elbow slightly bent and locked, and the left arm out in front pointing toward the target, I hand toss balls to them. I have them position the racquet so the balls just bounce off the racquet. In essence, they are learning the block volley.

3. Next, I teach them the punch volley. With the wrist locked, the elbow bent slightly and locked, and the racquet slightly open, players cross-step with their left foot at a 45-degree angle toward the net. With the left arm out in front, the players use a short punchstroke, slightly high to low to produce backspin, using shoulder movement only.

Once players have the basic mechanics down, we proceed to the *Cooperative Volley Game* and the *Cooperative Two-Touch Volley Game* (see page 70). I participate so I can give constant feedback to the players regarding their technique.

Coaching Tips

There is no question that when hitting volleys, simplest is best and less is more. I emphasize to players that if they use proper technique, with good footwork and body position, they can be successful hitting volleys if they use minimal racquet movement.

Players' Tips

It is almost impossible to self-teach how to hit volleys properly. You need to learn proper volley technique from a knowledgeable friend or take lessons from a good instructor.

Teaching Backhand Volleys

The most important step is to decide that you will teach your players to hit a one-handed backhand volley. Many players, especially girls, learn and use the awkward and self-limiting two-handed backhand volley. Not only does this shot look bad, it often performs badly.

1. I teach the neutral position in this way: Right hand with the continental grip (short to start), left hand with thumb, index finger, and middle finger on the bottom part of the frame. The racquet is exactly vertical and neutral. The top of the racquet is just below the eyes, because it is difficult and unnecessary to track an incoming ball with the racquet in the visual path.

2. Players start with a shortened continental grip for all-important racquet control. I have them start by positioning the racquet slightly in front and to the left side. With the wrist locked, the elbow slightly bent and locked, and the left hand still on the racquet, I hand toss balls to them. I have them release the left hand and extend the left arm backward, just before letting the ball simply bounce off the racquet, in essence, the block volley.

3. Next, I teach them the punch volley. With the wrist locked, the elbow bent slightly and locked, and the racquet slightly open, players cross-step with their right foot at a 45-degree angle toward the net. The left hand stays on the racquet until just before ball impact. At that point, players release the left hand and extend the left arm backward, just before using a short punch stroke, slightly high to low to produce backspin, using shoulder movement only.

Once players have learned and demonstrated the correct mechanics, we proceed to the *Cooperative Volley Game* and the *Cooperative Two-Touch Volley Game* (see page 70). I participate so I can give constant feedback to the players regarding their technique.

Coaching Tips

When novice or intermediate players show up for their freshman season with an entrenched two-hand backhand volley, it is usually a battle to get them to change to a one-hand technique. Many girls will say emphatically, "I can't do that," but what they really mean is "I won't do that." Players with an open mind and an ambitious mentality quickly learn this technical skill, and they have the opportunity to improve this shot so it is a real weapon, rather than a liability.

Several years ago, I witnessed a girl from another school lose a big singles match, solely because she used an awkward two-hand backhand volley, with a partial swinging motion. In this match, she dominated from the baseline, but when she got to the net (which was frequently) and played a volley from her backhand side (which was frequently), she had a huge error rate, and it led to her downfall.

Help your players understand that not only is the one-hand backhand volley an effective shot, it is also one of the prettiest shots in tennis. Perhaps visualizing their court appearance will motivate some players to learn the techniques to produce this shot.

Players' Tips

It is almost impossible to self-teach how to hit volleys properly. You need to learn proper volley technique from a knowledgeable friend or take lessons from a good instructor. Many self-taught players manage to get by with a mediocre forehand volley because of athletic skills, but the self-taught one-hand backhand volley is usually not a work of art or a success.

Teaching the Serve

1. Have players start with a short continental grip and serve from the service line, with the racquet starting in the "cocked" position.

2. The ball toss is exceedingly important for serve development, and players must learn good toss technique. The ball is held by the thumbtip and fingertips, with wrist and elbow joints locked, and movement is only at the shoulder joint. In essence, the tossing arm should be like a "robot arm"—a smooth swing upward and a clean release of the ball by simply opening the fingers and thumb, so it reaches a height about 4–6 inches above the top of the outstretched racquet.

The serve after completion of the toss

3. In my experience, about half of novice players have earlier success with the flat serve, and about half have earlier success with the slice serve. Very few have early success with the topspin serve. As a result I alternate serve instruction and practice between the flat and the slice serves until the players have reasonable consistency in at least one of these. Then I introduce the topspin serve.

4. When teaching the flat serve, I have players shadow drill the pronation snap repeatedly before they try to hit a ball. The toss should be about 12 inches in front of the left foot.

5. When teaching the slice serve, I have players shadow drill brushing across the ball at the 4 o'clock mark repeatedly (this gives the serve mostly side spin, with some topspin, which is a nice combination) before they try to hit a ball. The toss should be about 12 inches in front of and 4 inches to the right of the left foot.

6. When teaching the topspin serve, I have players shadow drill, brushing straight up under the ball at the 6 o'clock mark repeatedly before they try to hit a ball. The toss should be above the head. By leaning back-

ward at the knees, the players can look up at the ball and swing their racquets straight up under it to hit with topspin.

7. After multiple serves from the service line, I have them move back to an imaginary line half the distance from the the service line to the baseline, lengthen their grip to the half-way point, and hit more serves. Eventually, I have the players move to the baseline and use a full-length grip.

8. In a serving practice session for novices, each player may serve 20–40 balls from each of the three above lines.

Teaching the Forehand Slice

1. Players should initially use a shortened continental grip for maximum racquet control and gradually lengthen their grip as they improve their ability to hit this shot.

2. Players start in a neutral position, facing the net, with the left thumb and several fingers on the throat of the racquet. They start their take back to shoulder height

The forehand slice

with the racquet in a slightly open position. The wrist is locked and the elbow is slightly bent and locked.

3. Players release the left hand and extend the left arm forward toward the target. Step toward the target with the left foot and leg, and drive the racquet down an imaginary inclined plane to hit behind and slightly under the ball, imparting backspin while driving through the ball, using shoulder movement only until after contact with the ball.

4. If players use a glide step (sometimes called a slide step or sideways shuffle step) in setting up to hit this shot, it adds rhythm and power to the shot.

5. Use a full follow-through, which is important to impart significant pace and spin to the ball.

Coaching Tips

The pro singles players rarely use a forehand slice. Typically they use it only as a defensive save shot when they are pulled out wide to the forehand side and cannot set up for a forehand topspin. However, the forehand slice as a change-up from the baseline, and the forehand slice as an approach shot can be effective in singles play at the high school level. In particular, the inside-out forehand slice with sidespin added can be a terrific approach shot to the opponent's backhand, because it stays low and spins away. Thus it is a tough ball to lob and a tough ball to optimally time for a passing shot.

Doubles players at all levels use the forehand slice as an approach shot and as a return of serve before moving to the net, because it tends to stay low. Thus, it is a tough ball to lob. The inside-out forehand slice approach with side spin added from the ad court is a killer shot in doubles.

Several years ago during a practice session, I started to teach our four varsity singles players the technical aspects of the forehand and backhand slice shots. Our top singles player, a junior, announced clearly, "Coach G, I don't do slices." And indeed she didn't, until a year later when she realized that quality slice shots were a positive addition to her singles play. Currently, as a successful D-3 singles and doubles player, she has mastered both forehand and backhand slices and uses them to great effect.

Players' Tips

This is a wonderful shot to learn and master, but you must learn it correctly, and this means learning it from a good instructor or a skilled friend who is willing and able to teach this shot.

Teaching the Backhand Slice

1. Players should initially use a shortened continental grip for maximum racquet control and gradually lengthen their grip as they improve their ability to hit this shot.

2. Players start in a neutral position, facing the net, with the left thumb and several fingers on the throat of the racquet. They start their take back to shoulder height, with the racquet in a slightly open position. The wrist is locked, and the elbow is slightly bent and locked.

3. Players release the left hand and extend the left arm backward, symmetrically but opposite to the racquet going forward. Step toward the target with the right foot and leg. Drive the racquet down an imaginary inclined plane to hit behind and slightly under the ball, imparting backspin while driving through the ball, using shoulder movement only until after contact with the ball.

4. If players use a glide step (sometimes called a slide step or sideways shuffle step) in setting up to hit this shot, it adds rhythm and power to the shot.

5. Use a full follow-through, which is important to impart significant pace and spin to the ball.

Coaching Tips

Pro singles players now use the backhand slice extensively as part of their baseline rally strategy to give their opponents a change of pace and spin. Singles players also use this as a defensive shot when pulled wide to the backhand side without time to set up to hit a backhand topspin shot.

Doubles players at all levels use this shot as an approach shot and as a return of serve before moving to the net, because it tends to stay low. Thus, it is a tough ball to lob. The inside-out backhand slice approach with side spin added from the deuce court is a potent weapon to use in doubles.

Players' Tips

This is an important shot to learn and master, but you must learn it correctly, and this means learning it from a good instructor or a skilled friend.

10 Mini-Tennis Provides High-Level Training Games

I t makes sense to start a practice session with competitive mini-tennis games, which are a nice way to transition from the 10-minute session of warm-ups, balance drills, and stretching to full-court games.

A top mini-tennis player must possess excellent racquet control, ball control, and footwork, which are all requisites for successfully playing full-court tennis.

I detail some mini-tennis games that provide tremendous training for beginning, intermediate, and advanced players.

In each scenario, the coach states the game and the specific rules for the game. Each game will last until the coach calls time, typically at 2–3 minutes, or until a specified winning score is reached.

The coach may choose to put a greater or lesser emphasis on winning and losing these games, by designating or not designating rewards and/or penalties for the winners and losers.

If the coach chooses to emphasize winning and losing, then winners are exempt from the designated exercise that the losers must do (such as 2–5 pushups, one of a number of core exercises, a short sprint to the outer fence and back, a split-step drill, etc.).

Two simultaneous 1 v 1 mini-tennis games

These mini-tennis games, with four on a court, can be structured so that play is 1 v 1 or 2 v 2. In 1 v 1 games, each player gets a high number of reps per minute, whereas in 2 v 2 games, the number of reps per player per minute are typically half as many.

The level of precision required in 1 v 1 is significantly greater than that required when playing 2 v 2, because the target area in 1 v 1 is half as large as in 2 v 2. The ability to hit the ball with precision is an essential tennis skill, and if players become proficient in hitting with precision during mini-tennis games, this will certainly carry over to full-court play.

I suggest that players compete in the 1 v 1 format 80–90% of the time, and compete in 2 v 2 and 3 v 3 about 10–20% of the time.

Coaching Tips

In each of these games, players are allowed—and encouraged—to move to the net to hit volleys (and overheads, if their opponent attempts to lob inside the service line, which is a difficult shot). If there is a shot restriction in place, that restriction is waived once the player is at or inside the ideal volley position (IVP = halfway between the net and the service line). This is essential to help novice, intermediate, and some advanced players acquire experience coming in to the net to volley under less threatening circumstances than when their opponent is blasting away from the baseline.

Instruct novice players to hold their racquet with a shortened grip, which helps them improve their racquet control and, thus, ball control.

Players' Tips

These mini-tennis games sharpen your shot precision, your spin control, and your footwork. Dedicate the first few minutes of your practice session to all-out competitive mini-tennis and you will find it challenging. You will be rewarded with enhanced skill and confidence when handling balls inside the service line, and your precision both inside and outside the service line will improve as well.

Parents' Tips

If you see your child spending significant amounts of time during lessons or practice sessions playing mini-tennis, you will now understand how important these games are to his or her tennis development.

Game 1: Any Shot Goes

The Setup (this is referred to as the Mini-Tennis Prototype in subsequent games):

1. Four players on a court, playing 2 separate games of 1 v 1. Two games are going on simultaneously on the same court, which maximizes court usage and ball touches per player per practice hour.

2. If the players are all singles players, they can use either half the width of the singles court or half the width of the doubles court. (Coach's decision: A higher level of precision is required if using half the width of the singles court, and this is suitable for more advanced singles players.) If they are all doubles players, they will use half the width of the doubles court. Court depth is to the service line.

3. Players on one side of the court have a common ball hopper to feed from, and those two players both feed and keep score.

4. If the player is at or inside the IVP, they can hit any volley or overhead shot.

5. The coach starts each game, and the game ends when the coach calls time or when the winner reaches a specified score. When the game is over, the coach requests a show of winners, and may choose a reward for the winners and a penalty for the losers.

Version 1

Each player hits to half the width of the doubles court or to half the width of the singles court to the service line, straight ahead, with any shot allowed. (See page 59.)

Version 2

Each player hits to half the width of the doubles court or to half the width of the singles court to the service line, crosscourt, with any shot allowed. (See page 59.)

Version 3

The 4 players switch from deuce to ad, and ad to deuce. After this switch, the coach may have either the deuce players switch sides or the ad players switch sides to create the most variety possible in match-ups.

Each player hits to half the width of the doubles court or to half the width of the singles court to the service line, straight ahead, with any shot allowed. (See page 60.)

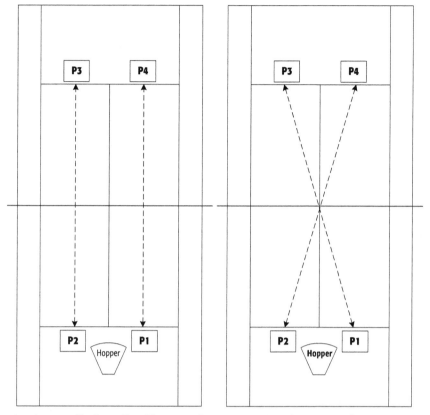

Any shot goes, Version 1 (P1 = Player 1, etc.)   Any shot goes, Version 2

Version 4

The players remain in the same position as Version 3. Each player hits to half the width of the doubles court or to half the width of the singles court to the service line, cross-court, with any shot allowed. (See page 60.)

Coaching Tips

Each of the 4 players gets a high number of reps hitting from the deuce side, both straight ahead and cross-court, and from the ad side, both straight ahead and cross-court. This helps players develop all their shots and become well-rounded players who can attack and defend from all parts of the court.

Left to their own inclinations, players tend to find a comfortable area of the court to hit from and comfortable shots

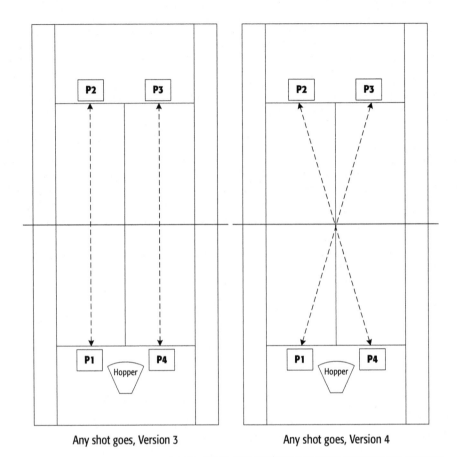

Any shot goes, Version 3   Any shot goes, Version 4

to hit. They tend to avoid uncomfortable parts of the court and uncomfortable shots.

Players' Tips

This forces players, who may be veterans set in their ways, to expand their games, get out of their comfort zones, and work on angled shots, touch shots, and net play. This improved play inside the service line is especially valuable for doubles players.

Game 2: Forehand Topspin Shots Only

The Setup: Use the Mini-Tennis Prototype.

1. Players can only hit forehand topspin shots, unless they are at or inside the IVP.

2. Follow the court positions and shot directions in Versions 1–4, in Game 1.

Coaching Tips

Novice players need frequent reminders to use the semi-western grip (with the second MCP joint on the #4 bevel) for the forehand topspin shots. If they use a shortened grip, they are able to generate more racquet and ball control when playing these games. Players get a high number of competitive reps, hitting all the standard forehand topspin shots: down the line, cross-court (including tight-angle cross-court), inside out, and pull (also called the inside in). There are opportunities to get to the IVP and finish the point with a volley. This game, with one shot type only, requires good footwork and anticipation to be consistently successful.

Players' Tips

Push yourself and your playing partner to be consistent, which leads to long forehand topspin rallies. Look for opportunities to move toward the net to hit a finishing volley.

Game 3: Backhand Topspin Shots Only

The Setup: Use the Mini-Tennis Prototype.

1. Players can only hit backhand topspin shots unless they are at or inside the IVP.
2. Follow the court positions and shot directions in Versions 1–4, in Game 1.

Coaching Tips

Less skilled players need frequent reminders to use the correct grips for the two-hand backhand topspin. (I favor the dominant hand with the second MCP joint at the 1.5 bevel, and the nondominant hand with the second MCP joint on bevel #4, counting in the opposite direction.) If they use a shortened grip, they can generate more racquet and ball control when playing these games.

Players get a high number of competitive reps hitting all the standard backhand topspin shots: down the line, cross-court (including tight-angle cross-court), inside out, and pull (or inside in). There are opportunities to get to the IVP and finish the point with a volley. To be consistently successful, this game, with only one shot type, requires good footwork and anticipation.

Players' Tips

Push yourself and your playing partner to engage in long backhand topspin rallies. Look for opportunities to move to the net to hit a finishing volley.

Game 4: Forehand Slice Shots Only

The Setup: Use the Mini-Tennis Prototype.

1. Players can only hit forehand slices unless they are at or inside the IVP.
2. Follow the court positions and shot directions in Versions 1–4, in Game 1.

Coaching Tips

It is essential for players to use the continental grip for forehand slices as well as using proper footwork. Stepping into the shot with the lead foot (left foot for a right-handed player hitting a forehand slice) provides power and direction. Less skilled and weaker players should use a short continental grip to attain better racquet and ball control.

Players get a high number of competitive reps hitting all the standard forehand slice shots: down the line, cross-court (including tight-angle cross-court), inside out, and pull. There are opportunities to get to the IVP and finish the point with a volley. To be consistently successful, this game, with one shot type only, requires good footwork and anticipation. The slice shot repetitions are valuable for players hitting balls in the midcourt and for hitting effective approach shots in both singles and doubles.

Players' Tips

Push yourself and your playing partner to engage in long forehand slice rallies. Look for opportunities to move to the net to hit a finishing volley. With excellent footwork and many reps, the forehand slice becomes a valuable weapon in the midcourt in both singles and doubles, and most valuable as an effective approach shot.

Game 5: Backhand Slice Shots Only

The Setup: Use the Mini-Tennis Prototype.

1. Players can only hit backhand slices unless they are at or inside the IVP.

2. Follow the court positions and shot directions in Versions 1–4, in Game 1.

Coaching Tips

It is essential for players to use the continental grip for backhand slices as well as using proper footwork. Stepping into the shot with the lead foot (right foot for a right-handed player hitting a backhand slice) provides power and direction. Less skilled and weaker players should use a shortened continental grip to attain better racquet and ball control.

Players get a high number of competitive reps hitting all the standard backhand slice shots: down the line, cross-court (including tight-angle cross-court), inside out, and pull. There are opportunities to get to the IVP and finish the point with a volley. To be consistently successful, this game, with one shot type only, requires good footwork and anticipation. The slice shot repetitions are valuable for players hitting balls in the midcourt and for hitting effective approach shots in both singles and doubles.

Players' Tips

Push yourself and your playing partner to engage in long backhand slice rallies. Look for opportunities to move to the net to hit a finishing volley. With excellent footwork, and many reps, the backhand slice becomes a valuable weapon in the midcourt in both singles and doubles, and most valuable as an effective approach shot.

Games with Other Variations

There are a number of variations the coach can use. Games in which competing players use different strokes provide excellent training to learn how to handle different spins when they are hitting from the baseline.

The Setup: Use the Mini-Tennis Prototype.

1. Players can only hit the shot they are assigned unless they are at or inside the IVP.

2. Follow the court positions and shot directions in Versions 1–4, in Game 1.

3. It is efficient to have the players reverse the assigned shots halfway through each version of the game. Assign these shot combinations to competing players.

   - Any forehand shot vs. any backhand shot
   - Any topspin shot vs. any slice shot
   - Forehand topspin vs. backhand topspin
   - Forehand topspin vs. forehand slice
   - Forehand topspin vs. backhand slice
   - Backhand topspin vs. backhand slice
   - Backhand topspin vs. forehand slice
   - Forehand slice vs. backhand slice

11 Midcourt Games Are the Toughest Games

Most players are uncomfortable hitting shots in the midcourt. Midcourt shots are challenging, because they are typically more difficult to execute than a clean-angled volley winner from the net or a big topspin shot from the baseline.

To get to the net from the baseline, we have to go through the midcourt successfully. If we cannot get through the midcourt successfully on our journey to the net, we will not get there to knock off the pretty angled inside out backhand volley winner that we want to hit.

The solution to the midcourt blues is to compete in structured games that require players to hit a high number of quality midcourt shots. For this purpose, I created some specialized games that are fun, challenging, and perfect for gaining confidence in executing an array of midcourt shots.

The Service Line Game

I created this game to help players learn to hit half-volleys during competition. After learning the mechanics of the half-volley, most players don't use it because it is a difficult shot to master, requiring great touch and timing. Instead, when most players are coming through the midcourt and get a ball at their feet, they back up and play the ball off the bounce, in their strike zone, usually hitting a topspin shot. Their progress toward the ideal volley position is brought to a screeching halt, and even reversed as the player moves backward to hit this shot.

The solution I arrived at is: Do not let the player back up, which is a key rule in the Service Line Game.

The Setup

1. Each player must keep at least one foot on the service line. The player cannot move backward or forward to hit a ball unless the opponent hits a short ball that cannot be successfully hit from the service line on one bounce. In that special case, the player can move forward to hit the ball on one bounce, then must immediately return to the service line for the next shot.

2. The only shots that can be hit are the standard volley, the half-volley, the slice, and the overhead, so the continental grip is the only grip used.

3. If doubles players are playing 1 v 1 , the court size is half the width of the doubles court to the baseline, and if playing 2 v 2, the entire court to the baseline. Most games are cross-court for doubles players, since this best mimics doubles play. Games for singles players can be cross-court or straight ahead, using either half the width of the singles court or half the width of the doubles court.

4. If 4 players are on a court, there are typically 2 cross-court or straight ahead games occurring simultaneously, both 1 v 1.

5. If the opponent hits a lob, the player can hit an overhead if desired, but cannot leave the service line to get to the lob. This restriction puts a premium on keeping the ball low with backspin, so the opponent has difficulty hitting a successful lob.

6. Although players cannot move forward or backward, they can and must move laterally. This game provides

frequent opportunities for quick and balanced lateral movements, which are important footwork skills in the midcourt.

7. The feeder (typically one of the players, but this could be a coach) feeds balls of varying pace and position, but most feeds should require a volley or half-volley on the first ball.

8. The feeder or feeding team (if playing 2 v 2) has a hopper of balls and keeps score. The game goes until the coach calls time or until it reaches a pre-determined winning score (such as 5, 7, or 10) per coach's decision.

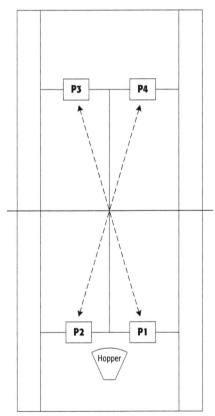

The Service Line Game, with two simultaneous 1 v 1 games

Coaching Tips

This game gives players a high number of reps in the midcourt hitting half-volleys, volleys, and slices, with the emphasis on keeping all shots low to prevent successful lobs. This game forces players to use good lateral footwork. 1 v 1 is the most efficient training game, and the coach should set up rotations so opponents change every game.

Players' Tips

1 v 1 games are best, but if you have an odd number of players, you can play 1 v 2 or 2 v 3, so no one sits out.

The Modified Service Line Game

The only changes in this modified game compared to the standard game are the shots allowed. Now players can use standard volleys, swinging volleys, half-volleys, slices, overheads, and topspin shots—any shot they want to hit. All other rules stay the same.

Coaching Tips and Players' Tips

This expands the options for midcourt shots, including swinging volleys on selected shots and topspin strokes on "sitters" (balls that bounce reasonably high). I believe it is beneficial for the average player to play the standard service line game almost exclusively, and for some of the advanced players to occasionally play the modified service line game.

The Competitive Volley Game

This game is excellent training for doubles players and singles players as well. It is a rapid-fire game that most players enjoy.

The Setup

1. All players start each point standing on the service line. One side feeds the first ball to start the point and keeps score. Served balls should vary in pace and placement.

2. Players may hit any shot. This game can be played as 1 v 1, 2 v 2, 3 v 3, or 4 v 4.

3. When playing 1 v 1, the court is half the width of the doubles court, playing either straight ahead or cross-court (the coach may limit singles players to half the width of the singles court, either straight ahead or cross-court) to the baseline.

4. All players must move forward after hitting their first volley (after the feed if the feeding player or team) until they reach the IVP or until the point is over. If players do not steadily move forward or if they move backward, they automatically lose the point.

5. The feeder or feeding team keeps score. The game goes until the coach calls time or until it reaches a pre-determined winning score (such as 5, 7, or 10) per coach's decision.

6. The coach designates rotations so players face a different opponent each game.

Coaching Tips

This game teaches players to constantly move forward when at or inside the service line, and includes a high number of reps of volleys, half-volleys, and other midcourt shots. It also teaches players to keep their shots low, since they cannot back up to go after lobs. It is more difficult to lob off a low slice or standard volley than off a shot that sits up.

Players' Tips

If there are two of you, rotate through all four possible games: Play from the deuce and ad sides, and play straight ahead and cross-court. If you play four consecutive games with intensity to 7, you will need a rest when you're done.

The Competitive Modified Volley Game,

The only change from The Competitive Volley Game is: All players start each point on the service line. Then players can go forward or backward as they choose.

Coaching Tips and Players' Tips

Players get a lot of reps in the midcourt but may retreat to defend against lobs, which is an important skill. Some players continually back up as the point develops because they are more comfortable at the baseline, and they may lose most points. This can be a teaching moment and a point of emphasis for the coach: The player moving forward typically wins this game, and the player retreating typically loses.

The Cooperative Volley Game
The Setup

1. Players (4–8) are on the same court, half on each side of the net, and all are at the IVP.

2. One player (or the coach) has a hopper of balls and starts the play with a soft volley to a player on the opposite side of the net.

3. The objective is to hit continuous controlled volleys, back and forth, using forehand and backhand volleys, with different angles, including all players on the court. If necessary, half-volleys can be used to keep the ball in play.

4. The players rotate one spot every 1–3 minutes, so they get reps from different spots on the court.

5. This is an ideal game for the coach to participate in. The coach feeds the first ball and provides instruction as needed.

6. This same game can also be played with all players on the service line. In this version, players need to learn to handle and hit longer volleys and half-volleys.

The Cooperative Two-Touch Volley Game
The Setup

1. All aspects are identical to The Cooperative Volley Game, except players must control the ball with the first touch, and hit a controlled volley with the second

touch. The first touch may be off a half-volley, if necessary.

2. If your players are skilled and good at this game, add another element of difficulty: The first and second touches must be from opposite sides. For example, the first touch for control is a forehand, and the second touch, the volley, must be a backhand. This additional requirement pushes your players to further develop their racquet and ball control.

3. This game can be played with all players on the service line.

Coaching Tips

I have been repeatedly surprised how difficult these two games are for reasonably skilled players, which tells me that many players do not have adequate footwork, body control, racquet control, or ball control to consistently hit quality volleys. In my experience, if I participate in these two games with our players, giving instruction and feedback when necessary, and give exercise penalties when warranted for repeated poor technique or focus (for example, 2 pushups), the dividends in terms of learning are significant.

Players' Tips

Do these two games with a friend or friends and discipline yourselves to use proper volley technique (the continental grip, locked wrist, slightly bent elbow which is locked, a short controlled punch motion from the shoulder only, a slightly open racquet face to impart backspin). Use different positions on the court to create different angles. You will love the results when you hit volleys in your matches.

12 Net vs. Baseline Games

2 at the Net vs. 2 at the Baseline, or 1 at the Net vs. 1 at the Baseline, with Innovative Variations

The net players always begin the point with a reasonable feed to the baseliners (unless the coach is feeding). Alternate the feed to one side or the other, or the middle, to give the baseliners roughly equal reps hitting forehand and backhand baseline shots. The net players always begin the points at the Ideal Volley Position (IVP) in the middle of the service boxes, and then must slide side-to-side to mirror the position of the ball at the baseline, to cover the potential baseline shot angles most effectively.

Version 1

The Setup

1. 2 v 2: The 2 net players feed to 2 baseliners (or the coach can feed) and keep score, and the point is played out.

2. The baseline players can hit any shot, including lobs. The net players can hit any shot.

3. The game is to a certain point total or to a time per the coach.

4. Players rotate after each game, and play 4 games total, so each player gets equal reps at all 4 positions.

Coaching Tips and Players' Tips

This game provides multiple reps for baseliners and net players in a competitive environment. Any shot is allowed, which matches the situation that might occur in a doubles match, with one team playing the defensive two-back formation, and one team taking control of the net.

Version 2

The Setup

1. One net player feeds to one baseliner. They play using either half the width of the doubles court or half the width of the singles court (this works well for singles players). Each point is played out, and the feeder keeps score. These games can be played straight ahead or cross-court.

2. The baseline players can hit any shot, including lobs. The net players can hit any shot.

3. The game is to a certain point total or to a time per the coach.

2 simultaneous games of 1 at the net vs. 1 at the baseline

4. Players rotate after each game, and play 4 games total, so each player gets equal reps at all 4 positions. This could include playing 4 games straight ahead, followed by playing 4 games cross-court.

Coaching Tips and Players' Tips

This 1 v 1 variation is a small- segment competitive game, where each player gets a high number of reps at each position in a short period of time. The number of touches per player per minute is a mark of the efficiency of this game.

Version 3

The Setup

1. The 2 net players feed to the 2 baseliners (or the coach can feed) and keep score.

2. The baseline players have shot restrictions: They can only hit topspin shots, and the shots have to be within 2 feet of the top of the net or they automatically lose the point.

3. The game is played to a certain point total or to a time per the coach.

4. Players rotate after each game, and play 4 games total.

Coaching Tips and Players' Tips

The purpose of this game is to teach doubles players to hit low topspin dippers when they are at the baseline and both their opponents are at the net. The topspin dippers force the net players to volley up, which might lead to an easy "sitter" (a ball that bounces medium height in the midcourt) for the baseliners. It also gives the net players opportunities to hit deft drop volleys.

   An excellent modification of this game is to restrict baseline shots to topspin shots that are within 2 feet of the top of the net, and also within 3 feet of the center of the net. This teaches doubles players that when they are at the baseline

and their opponents are at the net, the high percentage shot is usually low and over the middle. This brings the net players together, may create some confusion between the net players, and forces them to volley up.

This same game can also be played 1 v 1, either straight ahead or cross-court.

Version 4

The Setup

1. The 2 net players feed to the 2 baseliners (or the coach can feed) and keep score.

2. The baseline players have shot restrictions: They can only hit slices, and the shots have to be within 2 feet of the top of the net or they automatically lose the point. The players play out the point, playing 2 v 2.

3. The game is played to a certain point total or to a time per the coach.

4. Players rotate after each game, and play 4 games total.

Coaching Tips and Players' Tips

This game teaches baseliners to hit low slices, which can be difficult to volley successfully. It also teaches the net players to use a firm grip and excellent volley technique to handle the low backspin slice.

An excellent modification of this game is to restrict baseline shots to slice shots that are within 2 feet of the top of the net and within 3 feet of the center of the net. This teaches doubles players that when they are at the baseline and their opponents are at the net, the high percentage shot is often low and over the middle. This brings the net players together, may create some confusion between the net players, and forces them to volley up.

This same game can also be played 1 v 1, either straight ahead or cross-court.

The Third, Third, Third Game, Competitive

The Setup

1. The 2 net players, each positioned in the middle of a service box, feed to the 2 baseliners (or the coach can feed), and the point is played out. The feeders keep score.

2. The baseline players have shot restrictions: If the fed ball or returned ball is in the outer third of the court on either side, the baseliners have to hit a down-the-line shot. If the fed ball or returned ball is in the center third of the court, the baseliners have to hit a shot over the middle of the net.

3. The game is played to a certain point total or to a time per the coach.

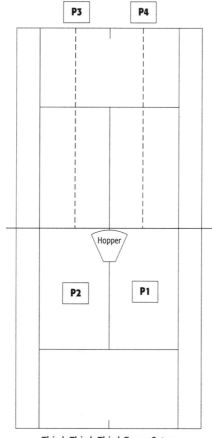

Third, Third, Third Game Setup

4. Players rotate after each game, and play 4 games total.

5. The coach can select additional shot restrictions for the baseline players:

   a. For intermediate and advanced doubles players, every shot has to be within 2 feet of the top of the net.

   b. Every shot has to be a topspin.

   c. Every shot has to be a slice.

   d. For intermediate and advanced doubles players, every shot has to be within 2 feet of the top of the net or it has to be a lob. Any shot in between results in automatic loss of the point.

Coaching Tips

In this competitive game, baseliners learn to hit down-the-line shots by being forced by the rules to do this repeatedly. This is a valuable skill to master in both singles and doubles. Players also learn to hit shots over the middle, which is a valuable option in doubles. Baseliners must hit low shots, including topspin dippers and low slices, which are valuable shots in doubles.

Baseliners must be able to hit successful topspin and slice lobs if their opponents are pressing the net. This forces at least one opponent off the net and creates open court opportunities for the baseliners.

It works nicely to do a round where the baseliners can hit topspin shots only so they concentrate on hitting low top-spin dippers, which are tough to volley. Next play a round where the baseliners can only hit slices so they concentrate on hitting low driving slices, which are difficult to volley.

The net players have to learn to slide side-to-side to cover down-the-line shots (by mirroring the position of the ball at the baseline). They also must learn to volley balls that barely clear the net by hitting touch drop volleys without popping them up as sitters. If lobs are allowed, net players must learn to backpedal quickly to hit overheads or retreat to play a deep lob and keep the ball in play.

Consider this terrific option for training doubles players. The coach allows two categories of shots: those that are only 2 feet above the net and lobs, either topspin or slice, depending on the type of shot allowed. Any shot in between these two heights is an automatic loss of the point. This perfectly fits the two heights of shots that should be used when a doubles team is at the baseline and their opponents are at the net, because the in-between shots in the "kill zone" get hammered.

Players' Tips

If there are 4 of you, you can play this exact game. If there are 2 of you, use half the width of the doubles court and play straight ahead. After one complete round of play, use the other half of the doubles court. The baseliner must hit balls on the outer fourth of the court down the line, and balls on the inner fourth of the court must go over the middle.

The Third, Third, Third Game, Cooperative

The Setup

This game can be played as a cooperative game rather than as a competitive game. The aim is to give baseline players reps in hitting precise shots. The net players can be instructed to hit manageable volleys and overheads back to the baseliners, rather than trying to hit winning volleys and overheads. The players rotate through all 4 positions based on time per the coach.

13 Baseline vs. Baseline Games:
Where the Big Hitters Like to Perform

Virtually all young players like to bash from the base-line, and they do need to develop this part of the game. In addition, we need to help them develop many more parts of the game to go along with this one important element.

I have created competitive games that help young players move beyond the baseline game. These games offer incentives and opportunities to move to a more sophisticated and fun level of play. At some point, most young players will be intrigued by the incentives and opportunities. They will attempt shots and tactics that would otherwise appear to be prohibitively intimidating or risky. If the game is structured properly, most competitive players eventually overcome their fears and attempt reps that help them move to a higher level of play.

Each game and its variations help the young players experience reps in different situations. This helps them expand their repertoires and become skilled, all-court players.

These games can be played as 1 v 1 or 2 v 2, or if need be, 1 v 2 or 2 v 3, with some minor adjustments of the parameters. 1 v 1 games, using half the width of the dou-bles or singles court with 4 players on a court, work beautifully and are my heavy favorite. Two separate games occur at the same time. This gives all four players on a single court a large number of competitive reps in a short time, which provides effective and efficient training.

Many of these games could fit under Chapter 15, Training Games for Singles Players. However, we know that many doubles players, especially early in their training, are more comfortable playing from the baseline rather than from the net. These games give doubles players reps from the baseline and encourage the players to move forward to get more comfortable at and inside the service line. Thus, many of these games could also fit under Chapter 14, Training Games for Doubles Players.

Players' Tips

Recreational and competitive players of all ages like to compete, and these half-court baseline games are perfect for intense competition and stroke improvement, but they eliminate much of the running. For players whose hips, knees, and ankles are less than pristine, elimination of excess running is a godsend. These players have left singles play behind and compete only in doubles. They find that these games using half the width of the doubles court provide opportunities to efficiently train for doubles competition, because good footwork and precision hitting are required to be successful.

Game 1, Forehand Topspin vs. Forehand Topspin, Version 1

Setup

1. Four players are on a court with 2 sets of 1 v 1 games going on simultaneously. All players start from the baseline. The players who have the hopper of balls on their side start the point with a reasonable underhand feed. They also keep score.

2. The court size is either half the width of the singles court or half the width of the doubles court. Players will play deuce to ad, i.e., straight ahead.

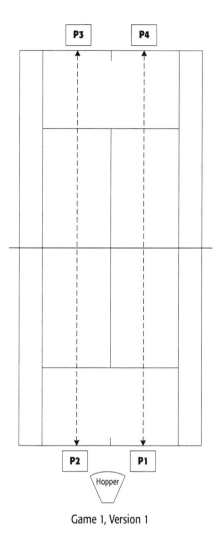

Game 1, Version 1

3. Only one type of shot is allowed: the forehand topspin, which can include the topspin drive, the topspin looper, and the topspin lob. If players hit any other shot, they automatically lose the point. Thus, the deuce side players are hitting all forehand topspin down-the-line shots, and the ad side players are hitting all pull (or inside in) forehand topspin shots.

4. An incentive is provided to entice players to the net. If the player is inside the service line and wins the point, he or she gets 3 points rather than 1.

5. Although the players can only use the designated shot when outside the service line, inside the service line,

players can use any shot they want: volleys, slices, top-spins, overheads, etc.

6. To get to the net, players who get a midcourt/short ball must use the designated shot as their approach shot. If the shot is the forehand topspin, the players get fore-hand topspin reps hitting from the baseline and reps using the forehand topspin as their approach shot.

7. The game is played to a designated number of points or it ends when the coach calls time.

Coaching Tips

Most novice and intermediate players play at the baseline and try to win points from there. Some of the bolder players, even with little experience, are attracted to the incentive of 3 points. They will get inside the service line to attempt to win the point from there. Once players experience some suc-cess inside the service line or watch their opponents experi-ence success, they will get there again and again. Thus, they will compile those precious training reps of moving toward the net to finish the point successfully.

This game forces players to get a high number of reps with a specific shot. This automatically helps them improve their weaknesses and improve their strengths.

For doubles players, hitting to only half the width of the doubles court helps them to win the 1 v 1 rallies that fre-quently occur in doubles matches.

For singles players, hitting to half the width of the doubles court requires more precision and consistency (half the width of the singles court is 13.5 feet, rather than 27 feet for the whole singles court, and adding the doubles alley of 4.5 feet comes to 18 feet). If singles players are limited to hitting to half the width of the singles court only (13.5 feet wide), this requires even more precision and consistency.

Many players express frustration at having to hit to a reduced width court, which is exactly the response we as coaches seek. This tells us clearly that it is difficult for the players, and we want to put our players into difficult and challenging situations during training sessions.

Beginning and intermediate singles players generally should hit to half the doubles court, so they will have more success and be able to sustain longer rallies. Advanced singles players should hit to half the doubles court at times and half the singles court other times so they can learn to sustain long rallies in narrow spaces.

After hitting to narrow spaces for awhile, many players beg to hit using the full court. When they are allowed to do this, the full court seems huge to them, and they are usually happy to be released from the "small court prison."

The 3-point premium for winning the point from inside the service line seems to provide adequate incentive for most players; however, this is a flexible number. If the coach perceives that the players are still reluctant to move forward, the coach can up the ante to a 4- or 5-point premium. If you have eager net rushers, you might want to limit the premium to 2 points.

Players' Tips

Whether you are a novice, intermediate, or advanced player, this 1 v 1 game pays great dividends as you develop increased precision in your baseline rallies. The 3-point premium encourages you to move toward the net to finish points from there.

Parents' Tips

You will enjoy and appreciate watching your child play singles to a much greater degree if you understand that while all singles points start with both players at the baseline, skilled and confident players seek opportunities to move through the midcourt to the net to finish the point with a volley or overhead.

Game 1: Version 2

The Setup: The same as Version 1, except:

- Players now play deuce to deuce, and ad to ad.
- The deuce side players hit only forehand topspin cross-court shots, and the ad side players hit only inside out forehand topspin shots.

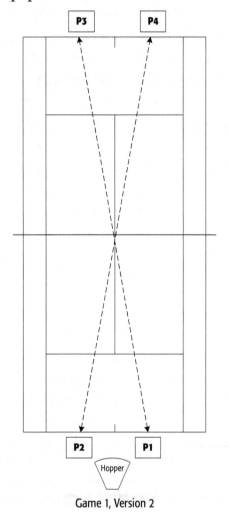

Game 1, Version 2

Game 1: Version 3

The Setup: The same as Version 1, except:

- Players trade court positions before starting this version (and remain there for Version 4). On each side of the court, the deuce player becomes the ad player, and vice versa. (The coach may have deuce players or ad players trade sides of the net to create an expanded variety of match-ups.)

- Players now play straight ahead, that is, deuce to ad, and ad to deuce.

- The deuce side players hit only forehand topspin down-the-line shots, and the ad side players hit only pull (inside in) forehand topspin shots.

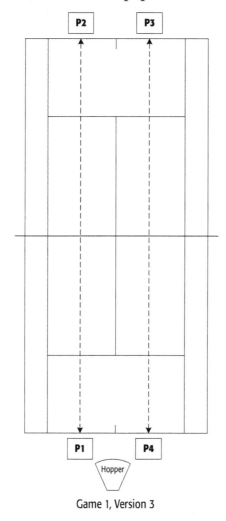

Game 1, Version 3

Game 1: Version 4

The Setup: The same as Version 1, except:

- Players now play deuce to deuce, and ad to ad.

- The deuce side players hit only forehand topspin cross-court shots, and the ad side players hit only inside out forehand topspin shots.

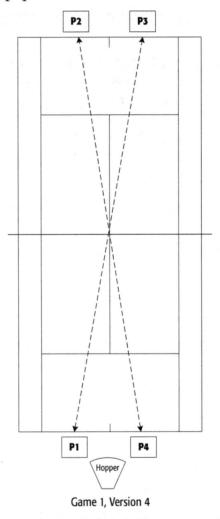

Game 1, Version 4

Coaching Tips

The 4 versions of this baseline game provide the repetitions and the competition to help your players. Whether they are beginners, intermediates, or advanced, they will develop and improve their 4 basic forehand topspin shots. These include down-the-line, cross-court, pull (inside in), and inside out, as well as the more difficult tight angle crosscourt and tight angle inside out shots. If the coach dedicates 2 minutes to each version, in 9–10 minutes all 4 players get a tremendous workout and a tremendous number of live-ball forehand top-spin reps. They hit a variety of forehand topspin approach shots, get a few opportunities to hit forehand topspin lobs, and may get a number of volley and overhead opportunities. Doing this sequence 1–3 times per week can only enhance your players' consistency and precision when using these shots.

Players' Tips

Discipline yourselves to do this rotational game at least occasionally as a substitute for match play. This helps you improve all your forehand topspin shots and no doubt improves your fitness, shot-making abilities, and precision.

Game 2: Backhand Topspin vs. Backhand Topspin
The Setup

Versions 1–4 are parallel to Versions 1–4 for Game 1, except players use the backhand topspin instead of the forehand topspin.

Coaching Tips and Players' Tips

Every one of these 4 basic backhand topspin shots from the baseline, plus the tight angle inside out and cross-court shots, is useful, although not necessarily during baseline rallies. Certainly the backhand topspin cross-court shots and the backhand topspin down-the-line shots are bread and butter baseline rally shots, but what about the other four?

Assume you are returning serve from the deuce court, and the serve comes to your backhand. If you can hit a big inside out backhand topspin drive return, a tight angle inside out backhand topspin return, or a big backhand topspin pull (inside in) return, these shots will pay huge dividends for both your singles and doubles game.

If you are playing singles, you may catch your opponent out of position when you hit these unexpected returns, because your opponent may expect a down-the-middle return. If you are playing doubles and hit a big pull return right at the opposing net player's midsection, you may win the point by inducing a volley error or a weak volley return. A tight angle inside out return causes the server (in singles or doubles) to go wide to get to the ball, which opens up a portion of the court for your next shot.

Assume you are returning serve from the ad court and the serve comes to your backhand. If you can hit a tight angle cross-court backhand topspin return, you cause the server (in singles or doubles) to go wide to get to the ball. This opens up a portion of the court for your next shot. Or, you return the serve to your backhand with a booming down-the-line backhand topspin return (in singles). You immediately put the server on the run and open up a large portion of the court for your next shot. If you hit the same return in doubles, right at the midsection of the net player, you may induce a volley error or a weak volley return.

As with the forehand topspin games, this series of backhand topspin games provides opportunities to hit backhand topspin approach shots and backhand topspin lobs as well as volleys and overheads.

Game 3: Forehand Slice vs. Forehand Slice

The Setup

Versions 1–4 are parallel to Versions 1–4 for Game 1, except players use the forehand slice instead of the forehand topspin.

Coaching Tips

Many players lack skill and precision with this shot and they tend to rely on the forehand topspin almost exclusively. However, at the middle school and high school level, a well-placed, low, skidding forehand slice can be a real weapon, especially as an approach shot in singles and doubles. This takes takes away the topspin lob as a passing shot and makes it more difficult to hit the other passing shots. This shot also provides an effective change of pace in a baseline topspin rally.

The inside-out forehand slice and the down-the-line forehand slice with side spin added are truly deadly approach shots if hit with depth, pace, precision, and significant back spin and side spin.

Players' Tips

Many older adult players hit more slice shots than topspin shots, which is certainly a generational difference. By playing the 4 versions of this game regularly, your forehand slice will become a more precise and lethal weapon.

Game 4: Backhand Slice vs. Backhand Slice
The Setup

Versions 1–4 are parallel to Versions 1–4 for Game 1, except players use the backhand slice instead of the forehand topspin.

Coaching Tips

If your players can master the backhand slice in all these versions, then they have a wonderful weapon to add to their arsenal of shots. This is especially true for approach shots in singles and doubles and for midcourt shots for doubles players.

The inside out backhand slice with sidespin added is a tough shot to master, but is also a tough shot to return.

Players' Tips

Many older adult players hit a backhand slice or a flat backhand shot, all one-handed, and do not hit a true backhand topspin shot. The four versions of this game help the older players improve their mastery of the backhand slice, which generally is a more effective shot than the flat backhand.

Games With Other Variations

- Any shot vs. any shot
- Any forehand vs. any backhand
- Any topspin vs. any slice
- Forehand topspin vs. backhand topspin
- Forehand topspin vs. forehand slice
- Forehand topspin vs. backhand slice
- Forehand slice vs. backhand slice
- Forehand slice vs. backhand topspin
- Backhand topspin vs. backhand slice

Coaching Tips

Put players into these structured baseline competitive games, with each player limited to one shot (but a different shot than the opponent). This gives players experience in the adjustments needed to hit against different spins and paces. Have the players switch shots halfway through the game. Have them rotate positions on the court and directions of shots as per usual.

These unusual formats provide variety that keeps players interested in competing during those mid- and late-season practices when interest sometimes wanes more than a little.

Players' Tips

Try all these variations. If one or more seem especially exciting to you and your friends, stick with it until you improve. This will pay dividends in your match play.

14 Training Games for Doubles Players

Almost every type of tennis training game or activity helps singles players and doubles players improve. However, some specialized games tailored to doubles players pay big dividends. In these games doubles players get a high number of reps of the most important shots used in doubles play, which should lead to improved success in matches.

Coaching Tips and Player's Tips

A key point to stress to doubles players: Keep the ball low, unless hitting a quality topspin lob or slice lob.

If our doubles team puts a low shot into the tape or net and loses the point, the result is one negative thing—the loss of one point. However, if our doubles team puts a floater up in the air at medium height and the opponents hammer it for a winner, the result is three negative things. The opponents feel great, our team feels lousy, and our team loses one point.

Parents' Tips

It is important for you to understand that doubles play differs markedly from singles play. The game of doubles is amazingly complex, and it is not easy for a casual observer to understand some of the intricate movements.

I have played, coached, and studied doubles play for many years, and I find that I continue to learn important things about doubles tennis.

The Modified Doubles Game, Version 1

The primary reason I created this game was to help players improve on their return of serve (ROS). This game also creates wonderful opportunities to teach multiple aspects of doubles play.

The Setup

1. The coach has a hopper of balls placed a few feet behind the service T, and the coach does all the serving from the service line. The coach plays out the points from the service line unless required to move to retrieve a ball, then returns to the service line. Points are played when the serve is good, and no points are awarded if the coach double-faults.

2. Three players are on the court, in standard doubles positions, with one being the coach's partner. Players rotate one spot after every 4 points. If there are more than 3 players involved, those sitting out rotate in every 4 points.

3. Each player competes against the other players in a race to accumulate a specified number of points to win, for example, the first one to reach 10 points. The coach decides on a reward for the one winner and a penalty for the game's losers.

4. The coach serves to the returner, who must return cross-court. If the cross-court return is successful, the 3 players and coach play out the point. Each player on the team that wins that point gets 1 point (the coach does not accumulate points). If the return is not cross-court, the serving team wins the point.

The coach serves 2 points in a row to be returned cross-court and played out. The coach then serves 2 points in a row to be returned down the line and played out.

After those 4 points are played out, a new player rotates to the returner position and the other players rotate positions.

The coach should use serves with the proper pace, spin, and location to suit the skill level of each returner. The coach serves to a specific location to the forehand or backhand side so the returner gets the reps needed to expand his or her ROS skills. Ideally, for the two cross-court returns, one serve is to the returner's forehand side and one serve is to the backhand side, repeating the same pattern for the two down-the-line returns.

With the coach serving from the service line, virtually every serve is in the service box, with the pace and location desired. This makes for a super-efficient and fast-moving game, without the wasted time of missed serves that are more common when serving from the baseline.

The coach should emphasize the important elements of ROS:

- Tight focus on the ball rather than on the server
- A split-step as the server's racquet moves forward
- Short, quick steps to get to the optimal return position
- A compact swing

The returner has less time to see and react to the ball when it is served from the service line. As a result of doing many ROS reps in this game, doing ROS when the server is at the baseline will seem comparatively easy.

5. A key feature of this game is that the coach awards bonus points for exemplary shots, footwork, effort, or team play, which provides extra incentives for players.

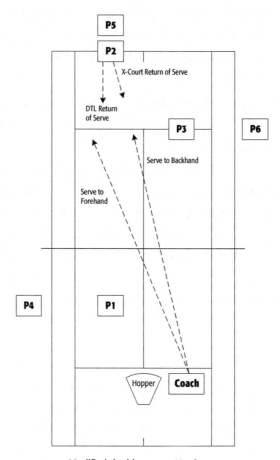

Modified doubles game, Version 1

6. On the flip side, the coach subtracts points for poor technique, poor effort, bad shot selection, or poor communication. This also provides extra incentives for players.

7. The coach dictates the type of ROS to use for a rotation (choosing one of 6 ROSs for the players to use: topspin drive, slice drive, block, topspin lob, slice lob, drop shot). Or the coach can let players use their ROS of choice.

8. At the end of a rotation (if the game started with the coach serving to the deuce court) when every player has had a turn at ROS, the coach serves to the ad court, and continues through the next full rotation.

9. These games, that end when 1 player reaches the win-

ning total (as 10 points), can continue for 30 minutes or more, if all players remain focused and enthusiastic.

Coaching Tips

This game is an exceptional way for the coach to help his or her players improve on ROS as well as other aspects of doubles play. It gives the coach a close-up view of each player's footwork, shot selection, and stroke techniques. It also gives the coach an opportunity to test players by hitting certain types of shots.

An option to consider: The coach can require the returner to hit the return, then move forward to the net until reaching the IVP or until the point is over.

This game works well if the coach is as good or better than the players. It will not work quite so well if the coach is a significantly lesser player than her or his players.

The first time I played this game with a group of six varsity doubles players, they were unsure about the scoring rules, so they played tentatively during the first few minutes. After a few points were played out, some bonus points were awarded, and some penalty points were subtracted, the intensity and focus picked up considerably. We played this game for 45 minutes straight because the girls were so enthusiastic and excited about it.

The same thing happened the first time I played this game with a group of 6 JV players. Their enthusiasm led to us playing the game for 40 minutes. I saw some extraordinary shots by these girls, because they all wanted to win bonus points.

When I play this game with high school boys, it works well. They add the element of happily attacking the coach when possible.

I have learned that although the practice plan may call for doing a certain game for only 15 minutes, if the game is going well, it is best to continue. It may be a rare top-level learning opportunity for our players.

Players' Tips

Instead of playing a standard doubles game, play this game for 20–30 minutes, rotating through all 4 positions. It will help your ROS game, your volley skills from the service line (as the server), and may surprisingly help your serving skills.

If desired, you can require the returner to move forward until reaching the IVP or until the point is over.

The Modified Doubles Game, Version 2

This is similar to Version 1, with these changes:

1. Four players are on the court at the same time, with one of the players serving from the service line, as the coach did in Version 1. If more than 4 players are in the game, those sitting out rotate in every change of position after 4 points are played.

2. The server gets serving reps from the service line, which is beneficial for serve development. A minor drawback to this version is that the serving players are not as nuanced as the coach would be in serving with proper pace, placement, and spin for the individual returner. The coach needs to instruct servers which pace to use to match the returner's skill level.

3. Each player keeps their own point totals. The serving team loses the point if the server double faults.

Coaching Tips

This version typically does not go as smoothly as Version 1, but it does get 4 players on the court. The server gets serving reps and also gets reps hitting half-volleys and volleys, etc., from the service line, which is valuable. This version of the game works better with more skilled players.

The coach watches the play closely and awards bonus and penalty points as deserved.

The coach can also require the returner to hit the return, then move in until reaching the IVP or until the point is over.

Players' Tips

This version is the same as Version 1. If desired, you can require the returner to move forward until reaching the IVP or until the point is over.

The Modified Doubles Game, Version 3

This version is similar to Version 1, with one major difference. Now the coach serves from the baseline. No points are played out until a serve is good, and no points are awarded for double faults.

Coaching Tips

Do not play this version unless you are a consistent server from the baseline, otherwise the game will be choppy and players may lose interest.

If desired, the coach can have the returner hit the return, then move forward until reaching the IVP or until the point is over.

Players' Tips

This version is similar to "real doubles," but there is still an emphasis on ROS. The rotation every 4 points adds to the novelty of this game.

If desired, the returner can be required to move forward after the ROS until reaching the IVP or until the point is over.

The Modified Doubles Game, Version 4

This version is almost the same as Version 2. The difference is that the serving player serves from the baseline. The serving team loses the point if the server double faults.

Coaching Tips

This version will typically not go as smoothly as Version 2, but it does get 4 players on the court at one time, and the server gets serving reps. Version 4 works better with more skilled players.

The coach watches the play closely and awards bonus and penalty points as deserved.

The coach can require the returner to hit the return, then move in until reaching the IVP or until the point is over. Also, the coach can require the server to serve and volley, moving forward until reaching the IVP or until the point is over.

Players' Tips

This version is exactly the same as Version 3. The returner can be required to move forward until reaching the IVP or until the point is over. Also, the server can be required to serve and volley, moving forward until reaching the IVP or until the point is over.

The 1 v 1 Doubles Game, Version 1

The Setup

1. Assign 4 players to a court, playing 2 games of 1 v 1. Players on one side have a hopper of balls. They serve from the baseline and keep score. The players on the opposite side return serve and the point is played out.

2. The game is cross-court, using half the width of the doubles court.

3. The two pairs may play points simultaneously, or may alternate playing points, per the coach's decision.

4. In this version, the players can choose to remain at the baseline or move forward.

5. Each rotation in this game lasts a specific number of

Two simultaneous games of 1 V 1 half-court doubles

points as designated by the coach, as 4–8 points for each pair. Then players rotate one spot. The game is done when each player has rotated through all 4 positions.

6. Each pair keeps their scores. At the end of the game, there will be 2 winners and 2 losers.

The 1 v 1 Doubles Game, Version 2
The Setup

This is similar to Version 1, except that the returner must move forward after the ROS and continue to move forward until reaching the IVP or until the point is over.

The 1 v 1 Doubles Game, Version 3
The Setup

This is similar to Version 1, except the server must move forward after the serve (serve and volley) and continue to move forward until reaching the IVP or the point is over.

The 1 v 1 Doubles Game, Version 4
The Setup

This is similar to Version 1, except the server must move forward after the serve (serve and volley), and the returner must move forward after the ROS. They both continue to move forward until they reach the IVP or the point is over.

Coaching Tips

These 4 versions are excellent games to help your doubles players enhance many of their doubles skills efficiently and productively.

Many doubles points are purely 1 v 1 affairs between the server and returner. They play out the point cross-court without any involvement of their partners.

Typically, the novice doubles players play out these points from the baseline. By using versions 2, 3, and 4, we can force our baseline-hugging players to move forward. With enough of these reps, our players become enthused about moving forward to be the aggressor and control the net.

The coach should emphasize to his or her players that it is difficult to win doubles points from the baseline; it is much easier to win points from the IVP.

Players' Tips

Play all 4 versions with your friends. You will grow increasingly skilled and confident at moving forward to win the point at the IVP.

15 Training Games for Singles Players

Almost every type of tennis training game or activity helps singles players and doubles players improve. Specialized games tailored to singles players are valuable, because singles players get a high number of reps doing what they have to do to be successful in their matches.

The Three-Shot Game

The Setup

This game is for intermediate to advanced singles players who have a reasonable mastery of forehand and backhand topspin drives, topspin loopers, and slices.

1. Assign 4 singles players to a court, playing 2 simultaneous 1 v 1 games using half the width of the singles court. The players focus on stroke production and precision, not on court coverage. Each player rotates through all 4 hitting positions, in the deuce court hitting straight ahead and cross-court, and in the ad court hitting straight ahead and cross-court.

2. The coach designates the 3 shots to be used in each set of 4 games: either 3 forehand shots (the forehand topspin drive, forehand topspin looper, and forehand slice) or 3 backhand shots (the backhand topspin drive,

backhand topspin looper, and backhand slice).

3. The coach designates the amount of time allotted to each version of this game.

4. Players on one side of the net have a hopper of balls and start the point with a reasonable underhand serve. Those players also keep score.

5. Of the 3 shots allowed, players cannot hit the same shot twice in a row. If they do, they automatically lose the point, unless they are inside the service line, in which case they can hit any shot.

6. Each ball served is worth 1 point, unless the winning player is inside the service line when the point ends, in which case it is worth 3 points.

Coaching Tips

The primary purpose of this game is to force singles players to use a variety of shots from the baseline. This helps them use change of pace and change of spin during baseline rallies in match play. In addition, players must concentrate on shot precision, and they have the option to move forward to win the 3 premium points.

Players' Tips

If you want to improve your ability to win long baseline rallies, put in some practice time using this game. You will be rewarded with improved command of these 6 shots. You will experience improved match performance due to your ability to mix up spins and pace to keep your opponent off balance.

The Shot Selection Game

The Setup

This game is for intermediate to advanced singles players who have a reasonable mastery of forehand and backhand topspin drives, topspin loopers, and slices. The coach runs this game because of the scoring and teaching aspects.

1. The coach is in the center of the service box on half the singles court with a hopper of balls. The coach starts the point with an underhand feed to a player at the baseline on half the singles court.

2. The player must hit the proper shot, depending on the location and type of ball he or she has to play. Their choices include hitting a topspin drive, a topspin looper, or a slice. The coach designates forehand shots only or backhand shots only.

3. The player should choose the proper shot based on these criteria:

   - **Topspin Drive:** Use this if the ball is near or inside the baseline and the player has time to set up to hit the ball in a comfortable strike zone.

   - **Topspin Looper:** Use this if the ball is at or behind the baseline and the player is moving backward to set up to hit the ball.

   - **Slice:** Use this if the player is running forward or sideways to reach the ball and does not have time to set up to hit a topspin drive or the ball is too low to allow a high percentage topspin drive.

3. Points scheme: If the player uses the proper shot and the coach can reach the shot to hit a return volley, that equals 3 points. If the player uses the proper shot and it lands in the half of the singles court the coach is on, that equals 1 point. If the player uses the wrong shot, that subtracts 1 point. If the ball bounces twice on the player's court after a volley or feed, that subtracts 1 point.

4. The player must reach a specific point total for the game to end, based on the coach's decision as to the player's skill level and fitness level. For example, an intermediate player might need to reach 8 points, and an advanced player might need to reach 15–20 points.

5. This game has 4 versions based on court positions of the player and coach: The coach is on the deuce half of

the singles court feeding to the player straight ahead and then cross-court. Then the coach is on the ad half of the court, feeding to the player straight ahead and then cross-court.

6. If the coach is working with 4 singles players and it takes 2 minutes per player per game, it will take about 32 minutes to progress through all the versions.

Coaching Tips

I created this game to teach one specific player to use better shot selection. This player loved to hit big topspin drives from any and every spot on the court when moving in any direction. As a result, she racked up a high number of unforced errors in each match. After using this training game during a number of practice sessions, the player's shot selection improved and, consequently, her match results improved.

Other singles players also showed improvement in shot selection, including some stubborn boys who resisted change until they found it took a long time to reach their designated point total. The light went on, they learned and adjusted, and their practice performance changed for the better. They showed remarkable improvement in their shot selection during subsequent match play.

This game is excellent for fitness training, since the coach feeds balls to keep the player continuously moving and hitting, stopping only to offer advice.

Players' Tips

Do this training game with a friend. Start with a realistic point target, such as 8 points. If you achieve easy success, move the point target higher until you are pushed to fatigue to reach it.

The Deep Shot vs. Deep Shot Game

The Setup

This game is for intermediate to advanced singles players who have reasonable mastery of forehand and backhand topspin drives, topspin loopers, topspin lobs, and slices.

1. 4 singles players engage in simultaneous 1 v 1 games using half the width of the singles court. The players focus on stroke production and precision, not on court coverage.

2. Each player rotates through all 4 hitting positions: in the deuce court hitting straight ahead and cross-court, and in the ad court hitting straight ahead and cross-court.

3. Each ball must land beyond the service line in the correct part of the court. If the ball does not land in the correct area, the point is lost.

4. The coach can limit the shots allowed to one shot only: forehand or backhand topspin drives, forehand or backhand topspin loopers, forehand or backhand topspin lobs, or forehand or backhand slices; any forehand shot; any backhand shot; or any shot.

5. Play is from the baseline only, since there are no short balls to use as an approach shot opportunity.

Coaching Tips

Note these important points:

- This game forces singles players to concentrate on all the factors important in consistently hitting the ball deep: increased knee bend, more height over the net, more topspin (if hitting topspin shots is allowed), and the proper pace.

- If players compete in this game regularly, they gain proficiency in keeping the ball deep and gain precision in their shot placement.

- Typically, after players compete in this game for 20 minutes restricted to one shot only, they beg for a change. They want the opportunity to hit to the entire half of the singles court, or to hit to the whole singles court; or to be allowed to hit any shot. By squeezing the players' target to a small area and limiting them to one shot type, we pressure them to be consistent and precise. This is difficult and frustrating for players, but also a valuable training experience. Later, when players are allowed to hit to an expanded court with an expanded arsenal of shots, they feel liberated.

Players' Tips

This game, especially with the limitation of one shot type only, is challenging and frustrating, but stick with it. This training game will pay big dividends in your singles' game.

The Vertical Game

The Setup

1. 4 singles players play simultaneous 1 v 1 games, using half the width of the singles court. They focus on stroke production and precision and on vertical court coverage, rather than horizontal court coverage.

2. Players rotate through all 4 versions of this game, hitting deuce to ad, deuce to deuce, ad to deuce, and ad to ad.

3. Players are allowed to hit 3 shots only: drop shots, topspin lobs, and overheads.

4. Players start at the baseline. One side has a hopper and gives their opponent a reasonable underhand feed to start the point. The side with the hopper keeps score.

5. The game goes to a specified number of points or until the coach calls time.

Coaching Tips and Players' Tips

If the players lack technical proficiency in the 3 shots used in this game, invest some time teaching or re-teaching these shots.

Singles players who master the vertical game can construct and execute points that put their opponent on the run—to the net to get to drop shots and then to the baseline to retrieve topspin lobs. If players hit high-quality shots, some drop shots and topspin lobs will be outright winners. If these shots do not go for outright winners, they force the opponent to do excessive running and drive the opponent to a state of frustration. An opponent who experiences the double whammy of fatigue and frustration is a beatable opponent.

Use overheads when the topspin lobs are short of their target.

The coach should consider limiting players to forehand or backhand drop shots and topspin lobs to force them to become proficient from both wings, because they typically favor one side over the other.

The Horizontal Game

The Setup

1. Three singles players are on a court, playing 1 v 2. The lone player is responsible for half the width of the singles court (the deuce half for the first complete rotation). The 2 players on the other side of the net are each responsible for half the width of the singles court.

2. The lone player has a hopper of balls, and starts the point with a reasonable underhand serve to one of the opposite players. The lone player keeps score, and the game goes to a specified winning point total or until the coach calls time.

3. The lone player must alternate hitting shots to the opposite deuce half and ad half. Failure to do this results in the automatic loss of the point. The opposing pair must hit every shot to the half of the singles court that the lone player is responsible to cover.

4. After each game, the players rotate one spot (if a fourth player is involved, that player rotates in), until all players have played a game at each position.

5. After a complete rotation, the players do a second rotation, with the lone player responsible for the ad half of the singles court.

Coaching Tips and Players' Tips

This game gives singles players valuable competitive repetitions in one basic singles tactic: moving the opponent from side to side. The lone singles player is only responsible for half the width of the singles court. This eliminates much of the running and allows this player to concentrate on alternating shots from one side to the other.

The ability to change the direction of an incoming ball, from cross-court to down-the-line, and vice versa, is a skill that is also honed in this game.

To enhance training opportunities, the coach has the option of allowing any shot, or restricting players to one shot only.

The Modified Singles Game, Version 1

The Setup

1. Four players are on a court, with the pairs playing a series of 1 v 1 games.

2. The court used is half the width of the singles court.

3. One side has a hopper of balls. That side serves and keeps score.

4. The 2 players on the serving side alternate serving points and playing them out.

5. The server on the deuce side serves 4 points (alternating points with the player serving from the ad side) and plays them out against the player on the opposite deuce court. The first 2 points are played cross-court, deuce to deuce. The third and fourth points start with the server serving from the deuce side, but the returner must hit a down-the-line return. The server plays the point out from the ad side.

6. The ad server does the mirror image of the deuce server.

7. After 4 points are played out by each pair, the 4 players rotate one spot and play the next game in the series.

8. After the 4-game series, there are 2 winners and 2 losers (16 points played per pair).

9. The next 4-game series could pit the 2 winners against each other, and the 2 losers against each other.

> ## Coaching Tips and Players' Tips
> This modified singles game accomplishes two objectives. First, it diminishes the court size and forces the players to be more precise in their shots. Second, it forces players to hit both cross-court and down-the-line ROS with some precision.

The Modified Singles Game, Version 2
The Setup

The same as in Version 1, except the returner has to move forward after the ROS and continue moving forward until reaching the IVP or until the point is over.

The Modified Singles Game, Version 3
The Setup

The same as in Version 1, except the server has to move forward after the serve (serve and volley) and continue moving forward until reaching the IVP or until the point is over.

The Modified Singles Game, Version 4
The Setup

The same as in Version 1, except the server has to move forward after the serve (serve and volley), and the returner has to move forward after the ROS. They both have to continue moving forward until reaching the IVP or until the point is over.

Coaching Tips and Players' Tips

If your singles players are intermediate to advanced and they perform well in Version 1, have them play Versions 2, 3, and 4 so they can experience repetitions in moving forward to finish points at the net.

---

16 Serve and Return of Serve: Incredibly Important

We know the serve is the most important shot in tennis, closely followed by the return of serve (ROS). We need creative ways to teach our players to be more effective when serving and returning serves. The methods must be interesting enough to hold their attention and must be constructed so players focus on the task at hand.

When I observe one player serving from a hopper and a partner returning those serves, I often see two problems. First, the server typically works too fast to focus on improving technique, pace, spin, and placement. Second, the returner often takes big, undisciplined cuts at the serves, without practicing the ROS intricacies.

I have observed that many coaches avoid teaching the ROS, because it is difficult and challenging to teach. However, if we break this teaching task into parts and use well-designed sequences and structures, we can help our players advance their ROS skills.

Think about this: If a singles or doubles player hits ROSs from the deuce court and works on only one of the 6 types of ROSs, for example the topspin drive, they need to learn to successfully hit 4 separate shots. These are the forehand topspin drive cross-court, the forehand topspin drive down-the-line, the inside out backhand topspin drive (to go cross-court), and the pull (or inside in) backhand topspin drive (to go down-the-line). From the ad side, they need to learn another 4 shots: the inside out forehand topspin drive, the pull (or inside in) forehand topspin drive, the cross-court backhand topspin drive, and the down-the-line backhand topspin drive. Thus, to return using a topspin drive, a player must master a staggering total of 8 ROS shots!

To master all 6 types of ROS (including topspin drive, slice drive, block, topspin lob, slice lob, and drop shot) from both sides of the court, as noted above, requires mastery of 48 separate ROS shots!

I devised structured games that teach ROSs and, at the same time, teach the serve.

The Cooperative Serve and Return of Serve Game, Version 1

The coach serves from the service line, with one or more hoppers of balls available.

The coach first teaches some key elements regarding the ROS, including proper positioning for a big first serve and for a lesser-paced second serve. The coach also teaches the proper method and time to split-step before the ROS.

The coach has the players use only one of the 6 types of ROS at a time. The coach reviews the proper way to hit the specific ROS and the strategy behind using it.

Each player gets an ROS rotation both from the deuce court and the ad court, giving the coach an opportunity to instruct each player.

Assume the coach is instructing 4 players, and the players are learning to hit the block return. The teaching goes as follows:

1. The coach presents the proper technique to hit a successful block return from both the forehand and backhand sides.

2. The coach serves 4 legal serves total to each player, who hits the ROS from the deuce court.
   - The player must hit the first 2 ROSs cross-court. The coach serves one to the forehand side and one to the backhand side.
   - The player must hit the next 2 ROSs down-the-line. The coach serves one to the forehand side and one to the backhand side.

3. After each of the 4 players has hit 4 ROSs from the deuce court, they do the same type of ROS from the ad court.

4. In 8 minutes or less, the coach can complete this cycle (assuming the coach is a consistent server). The coach serves with appropriate pace, spin, and location to match each player's ROS skills, and can give individual instructions as needed. This is an efficient and productive use of practice time.

Coaching Tips

This works well if the coach has mastery of serving from the service line (not that difficult to learn) and can teach the basics of at least 1 or 2 types of ROS, and preferably all 6 types.

Players' Tip

If players have mastery of serving from the service line, and at least one player knows how to do one or more types of ROS, this works beautifully for teaching each other.

The Cooperative Serve and Return of Serve Game, Version 2

The Setup

1. A player serves from the service line, with one or more hoppers of balls available. If there are 4 (or 5 or 6) players involved, one player serves from the deuce

service line, and another serves from the ad service line. The players serve alternately, not simultaneously, so a server is not hit with an ROS. The coach dictates the type of ROS to be used on every ROS for the full rotation.

2. The coach instructs the serving players to serve at a certain pace and spin, with every other serve going to the forehand, and every other serve going to the backhand.

3. As in version 1, the player hitting the ROS hits the first 2 cross-court and the next 2 down-the-line.

4. After each of the deuce and ad players have returned 4 legal serves, everyone rotates one spot. The process is repeated until each player has rotated to all 4 positions.

5. The coach may instruct the players to do a second full rotation with the same ROS or a different ROS.

Coaching Tips

If your players can stay on task, you can manage at least 2 courts of 4 each doing this game, and perhaps 3–6 courts. Each rotation of four players should take no more than about 8 minutes, so doing 1–2 rotations in a practice session does not take an inordinate amount of time. You may want to have your players concentrate on 1–2 types of ROSs only, for example, a block return for high-paced serves and a top-spin drive for slower serves. If you have talented players, they should learn the techniques and perform reps in 3–6 types of ROS.

The servers may not be able to accurately place the serve to alternate the backhand and forehand returns, but in repeatedly trying to do this, the players undoubtedly improve their control of serve placement.

Players' Tips

If there are 2 of you, do the same as in version 1. If you have 4 or more players, use version 2 with rotations.

The Competitive Serve and Return of Serve Game, Version 1

The Setup

1. The coach serves from the service line with a hopper of balls available. The coach remains at the service line to play out the point.

2. The player returns the serve and plays out the point, with the option of staying at the baseline or moving forward.

3. The coach may allow any type of ROS or specify a certain ROS.

4. The coach varies the serves' pace, spin, and location, depending on the returner's skill level. The coach alternates serves to each player to the forehand and backhand sides and gives immediate feedback to each player.

5. The coach could compete against the entire group of players or have each player compete against all the other players. This game goes to a specified number of points or minutes, per coach's decision.

6. For singles players, the game is played cross-court, using half the width of the singles court. For doubles players, the game is played cross-court, using half the width of the doubles court.

7. The coach may elect to have a group of players each play out 2 points and rotate, or have each player play out 4 points and rotate.

8. After playing to a designated score or time from the deuce court, the coach repeats the game from the ad court.

Coaching Tips

For this version to be successful, the coach must be reasonably adept at serving from the service line with the right amount of pace, spin, and location to challenge the players and allow them to return a high percentage of successful ROSs, creating the experience of playing out the point against an opponent at the service line.

Players' Tip

This is a great way for friends or teammates to improve ROSs and serves as well as playing out cross-court points.

The Competitive Serve and Return of Serve Game, Version 2

The Setup

1. Assume there are 4 players (it could be more) on a court. One player serves from the deuce service line, and one serves from the ad service line. The servers must stay at the service line to play out the point.

2. The returners hit the ROS and play out the point, with the option of staying at the baseline or moving forward.

3. The coach may allow any type of ROS or specify a certain ROS.

4. The coach instructs the serving players to vary the pace, spin, and location of serve, depending on the returners' skill level. The coach also instructs the serving players to alternate serves to the forehand and backhand.

5. Each 1 v 1 game goes to a specified number of points or specified number of minutes.

6. For singles players, the game is played cross-court using half the width of the singles court. For doubles players, the game is played cross-court using half the width of the doubles court.

7. The coach has the 4 (or more) players on a court rotate one spot, until all players have rotated to each of the 4 positions.

The competitive serve and return of serve game, Version 2

Coaching Tips

With cooperative and focused players, multiple courts can do this same competitive game at the same time, with players assigned to courts depending on their skill levels. The coach can have each 1 v 1 game last 2–3 minutes and, at the end of each game, reward winners and penalize losers as desired. The coach can roam, giving teaching instructions as needed.

Players' Tip

This is the same as Version 1.

The Competitive Serve and Return of Serve and Follow to the Net Game

This game benefits experienced players who have developed decent ROS and midcourt skills. For singles players and especially doubles players who like to play aggressively, this game creates reps to develop the skills needed to successfully return serves and win the point at the net.

Players can develop the foundation skills for this game by playing the *Service Line Game* and the *Competitive Serve and Return of Serve Game*.

The Setup

1. Assign 4 players to a court, with 2 servers serving from the service line, one on the deuce side and one on the ad side, and 2 returners, one on the deuce side and one on the ad side. For doubles players, the court is half the width of the doubles court. For singles players, the court is half the width of the singles court.

2. A server serves to a returner, the returner hits an ROS cross-court, and the point is played out. The coach may restrict the return to one type of ROS or allow any ROS. The returner must immediately move toward the net and continue moving forward until reaching the IVP or until the point is over. The server should alternate serves to the returner's forehand and backhand.

3. The server hits the serve and remains at the service line to play out the point. The server can retreat to cover lobs. This gives the server a large number of reps using midcourt shots, especially volleys and half-volleys.

4. Server-returner pairs play a specified number of total points, such as 8 or 10, with each player keeping score of their own winning points. Then the 4 players rotate one spot and repeat the exercise until a full rotation has been completed.

5. Server-returner pairs keep track of their own point totals through all the rotations. 2 players will win, and 2 players will lose.

6. If the coach has designated one type of ROS, after one full rotation the coach may designate a second ROS type. The coach designates a change in initial position

of the four players, so they compete against someone new.

> ## Coaching Tips and Players' Tips
>
> This game helps players learn multiple skills, including serve control and placement, ROS using different types of returns, moving to the net after ROS while using split-steps, hitting midcourt shots (both the server, who primarily stays at the service line, and the returner, who must move through the midcourt to get to the IVP), and hitting finishing volleys or overheads.
>
> If your players have difficulty executing the shots required in this game, stop the game and do some specific instruction on shot execution. Then let them try again. Many of the shots required in this game are difficult to master, such as ROS, half-volleys, and controlled volleys off high-paced balls. Players need time, repeated instruction, and a lot of reps to reach a moderate to advanced proficiency.

The 6-, 12-, and 18-Serve Game

The Setup

1. Four to 8 players are at the baseline, with 1–2 hoppers of balls. Each player hits a few serves to warm up.

2. Players who can hit only one type of serve (any type) do the 6-serve game; players who have mastered any 2 types of serve do the 12-serve game. Players who have mastered the basic 3 types of serve (flat, slice, and top-spin) do the 18-serve game.

3. Each player is their own judge of success or failure. Alternatively, players could be paired up to judge each other's serve success or failure.

4. To score a point when serving to the deuce box, each player must place a serve in the box. Additionally, the serve must land within 2 feet of each of 3 intended targets: down the middle, into the body, and out wide

with each type of serve used. The same applies when serving to the ad box.

5. Each player ends up with a score: for the novice, X out of 6; for the intermediate, X out of 12; and for the advanced, X out of 18.

6. It works well to have similar levels of players competing, but a mixture also works. If every player is at the same level, there is one winner; if it is a mixed group, there is one winner at each level.

Coaching Tips

We know it takes thousands of reps to master one type of serve. For a service rep to be helpful, the player must take the time to focus, use good mechanics, and set a goal. Often during serving practice, players rush each serve. They do not pay attention to the serve location or they hit every serve to the same general area. This game forces players to slow down and strive to reach a goal that requires consistency and precision.

Ideally, our novice players are able to hit one serve (flat or slice) with location (down the middle, into the body, or out wide), even though the pace may be on the slow side.

Ideally, our intermediate players are able to hit 2 serves (flat and slice) with location and at a moderate pace.

Ideally, our advanced players are able to hit 3 serves (flat, slice, and topspin) with location and at a significant pace.

Players' Tips

It is crucial to learn the continental grip and the proper mechanics for each of the serves, and to find the time and the motivation to do the reps. When you are practicing serves on your own, this game gives you a goal to strive for.

I have played with hundreds of adult players who clearly do not use the continental grip. They have some mastery over the location of a flat serve, and usually have some mastery over the location of a puffball second serve. They have reached a low-level plateau and will never improve unless they get some good instruction and are willing to learn the right techniques. Then they must put in some serious practice time to elevate their serve proficiency.

17 Specialty Shots:
Tough to Teach and Learn, But So Much Fun to Use

I have gone through much trial and error, seeking methods to effectively teach some of the specialty shots. I do not have perfect solutions, but I have developed some useful approaches that will enhance your chances for teaching success.

If we can help our athletes learn the basic technical aspects of a specialty shot and put them in the proper competitive practice situations, they will use their inherent athletic talents to develop mastery of that shot as they battle to win competitions.

Repetitions in a carefully constructed competitive game help players hone their consistency and precision and allow them to develop their own style of accomplishing the task of "owning the shot."

Important Note: The correct grip for many specialty shots, including the drop shot, drop volley, and overhead, is the continental grip, with the second MCP joint on bevel #2.

The Drop Shot, a Lovely Piece of Artistry on the Courts

If your players have mastered the technical aspects of the drop shot, move directly to the competitive game (next section).

1. Demonstrate how to put backspin on the ball, with the racquet held horizontally and with a short continental grip. Use a short forehand stroke to propel the ball upward 1–3 feet with significant backspin. Do this repeatedly without the ball touching the ground.

2. As soon as your players have spent 1–2 minutes practicing this maneuver, turn it into a competitive game. Each player tries to win the contest to hit the most repetitive ball control spins without letting the ball hit the ground in a 2–3 minute period. Good high school players can go over 100 consecutive ball control spins in that time.

3. Demonstrate the mirror image maneuver, using a short backhand stroke with a short continental grip. After your players have practiced this for 1–2 minutes, turn this into a competitive game, where each player tries to win the contest to hit the most repetitive ball control spins using the backhand stroke.

4. As your players gain proficiency at these games, have them gradually lengthen their continental grip.

5. Next, demonstrate the drop shot techniques, both forehand and backhand, from the service line. Emphasize extreme backspin, a soft touch, and nice height over the net for safety. Have your players do multiple shadow drills of both forehand and backhand drop shots.

6. In the next phase, hand toss balls to your players, who are at the service line. Have them each hit several forehand and backhand drop shots. Give them technical feedback as you do this.

The Competitive Drop Shot Game

The Setup

1. Assign 4 players to a court. There will be 2 simultaneous games of 1 v 1, service box to service box. Have the players alternate playing straight ahead, deuce to deuce, and ad to ad. Novice and intermediate players should use a short continental grip for increased rac-

quet and ball control. They can lengthen their grip as they gain skill in this shot.

2. Players on one side of the net start the point with an underhand feed and keep score. The coach determines the length of each game or if the players play to a certain score.

3. After the underhand feed to start the point, the only shots allowed are drop shots. The point is played out.

Coaching Tips

We know that to truly master the drop shot, it takes thousands of reps, great racquet control, and ball control. The teaching sequences above will certainly help novice and intermediate players with little or no skill in the drop shot. They can gain some proficiency with this shot in 30 minutes or less. A subset of these players, intrigued by the skill required and the artistry and effectiveness of this shot, will pursue perfection or near perfection on their own. To the coach's surprise and delight, these players will start using this shot in practices and matches.

Players' Tips

It is difficult to self-teach this shot. It is certainly best to learn this from a good instructor or from a friend who has the skill to teach it.

The Drop Volley: More Artistry on the Court

If your players have mastered the technical aspects of the drop volley, move directly to the cooperative and competitive games.

1. Demonstrate to your players how to put backspin on the ball, with the racquet held in a horizontal position and with a short continental grip. Use a short forehand stroke to propel the ball upward 1–3 feet with significant backspin. Do this repeatedly without the ball touching the ground.

2. As soon as your players have spent 1–2 minutes practicing this maneuver, turn it into a competitive game. Each player tries to win the contest to hit the most repetitive ball control spins without letting the ball hit the ground in a 2–3 minute period. Good high school players can go over 100 balls in that time.

3. Demonstrate the mirror image maneuver using a short backhand stroke and with a short continental grip. After your players have practiced this for 1–2 minutes, turn this into a competitive game seeking the most repetitive ball control spins using the backhand stroke.

4. As your players gain proficiency at these games, have them gradually lengthen their continental grip.

5. Next, from the IVP, demonstrate to your players the actual drop volley technique, both forehand and backhand. Emphasize extreme backspin, a soft touch, and nice height over the net for safety. Have your players do multiple shadow drills of both forehand and backhand drop volley shots.

6. In the next phase, hand toss balls to your players, who are at the IVP, and have them each hit several forehand and backhand drop volley shots. Give them technical feedback as you do this.

The Cooperative Drop Volley Game
The Setup

1. Assign 4 players to a court, 2 at the baseline and 2 at the net at the IVP, playing 1 v 1, straight ahead, with each pair using half the width of the singles court.

2. The baseliners (this could be a coach) have a hopper of balls and feed moderately paced low balls to the net player who is directly opposite. The net player hits drop volleys.

3. The coach can observe, comment, and reteach technique.

4. Players rotate positions every 2–3 minutes until a complete rotation has occurred.

The Competitive Drop Volley Game

1. Assign 4 players to the court, 2 at the baseline and 2 at the net at the IVP, playing 1 v 1, straight ahead, with each pair using half the width of the singles court.

2. The net players have a hopper of balls. They start the point with an underhand feed to their opponent and they keep score.

3. The baseline players must hit low shots—no more than 2 feet above the net—or they lose the point. The coach can designate which shots to use, either topspin or slice or both. The net players must hit drop volleys only or they lose the point. The opponents play out the point, hitting only the allowed shots.

4. The game is played to a certain number of points or to a time specified by the coach. Then the players rotate, going through all four positions.

Coaching Tips and Players' Tips

If your players are just learning the drop volley, use the cooperative game. For more advanced players, the competitive game will be valuable.

Half-Volleys

Forehand Half-Volleys

1. Players should start with a short continental grip and lengthen the grip as they gain proficiency in this shot.

2. The contact point between the ball and racquet must be just above the court surface. The player must use deep knee bends to achieve this, while keeping the head and back erect.

3. Similar to forehand volley technique, the wrist must be locked, the elbow slightly flexed and locked, and the racquet face should be slightly open. If the incoming

Forehand half-volley ball contact position

ball has significant pace, a block half-volley works nicely. If the incoming ball is soft and slow, a punch half-volley is the correct shot to use.

4. The ball should just clear the net, with back spin. This is a touch shot, not a power shot.

Backhand Half-Volleys

1. Players should start with a short continental grip and lengthen the grip as they gain proficiency in this shot.

2. The contact point between the ball and racquet must be just above the court surface. The player must use deep knee bends to achieve this, while keeping the head and back erect.

3. Similar to backhand volley technique, the wrist must be locked, the elbow slightly flexed and locked, and the racquet face should be slightly open. If the incoming

ball has significant pace, a block half-volley works nicely. If the incoming ball is soft and slow, a punch half-volley is the correct shot to use.

4. The off arm should move opposite to the racquet arm, similar to the backhand volley technique.

5. The ball should just clear the net, with back spin. This is a touch shot, not a power shot.

Coaching Tips and Players' Tips

Every good doubles player must be proficient in both forehand and backhand half-volleys to successfully move through the midcourt en route to the IVP. Singles players who serve and volley, or who return serve and move to the net must also master this shot. In Chapter 11, competitive games that help players learn to use the half-volley under pressure include the Service Line Game, and the Modified Service Line Game. Once your players have learned the technical skills of the half-volleys, they should play these games to gain proficiency during competition.

Tight-Angle Slice Shots, Nice and Precise

This shot is valuable, especially in doubles. If your players have spent time learning the mechanics of the slice (see Chapter 9) and have played mini-tennis games using the forehand and backhand slice (see Chapter 10), they will have practiced a number of reps hitting these tight-angle shots.

Tight-Angle Topspin Shots, Pretty and Precise

This shot is valuable, especially in singles. If your players have spent time learning the mechanics of the topspin (see Chapter 9) and have played mini-tennis games using forehand and backhand topspin shots (see Chapter 10), they will have practiced a number of reps hitting these tight-angle shots.

Topspin Lobs, a Potent Offensive Weapon

When a singles player or a doubles team presses too tightly to the net, and the opponent hits a topspin lob over the top that lands deep in the court and spins away into the fence for an outright winner, it is a beautiful sight. This winning shot requires excellent technique and extraordinary precision.

Forehand Topspin Lobs

If your players have mastered the technical aspects of this shot, skip this section.

1. Novice and intermediate players should start with a shortened semi-Western forehand grip and use the pull-up (reverse forehand) method, while leaning back slightly, to hit the ball with severe topspin. The shot should be high enough to clear the opponent's outstretched racquet.

The finish position for the forehand topspin lob

2. Have your players shadow drill this shot multiple times.

3. Hand toss balls to your players who are at the baseline. Carefully instruct and correct them as they learn this shot.

4. Once they learn the shot, teach them how to incorporate deception, since deception is vital to the success of this shot. Players should give off strong body and racquet signals to their opponent(s) that they will hit a topspin drive. At the last instant, the player leans back and hits the topspin lob. This deception freezes the opponent(s) at the net.

Backhand Topspin Lobs

If your players have mastered the technical aspects of this shot, skip this section.

1. Novice and intermediate players should start with a shortened two-hand backhand grip for increased racquet and ball control. They brush up behind the ball with the racquet climbing steeply to hit with extreme topspin, hitting the ball high enough to clear the opponent's outstretched racquet. They should finish with one arm on each side of the head, while leaning back slightly.

2. Have your players shadow drill this shot multiple times.

3. Hand toss balls to your players at the baseline. Carefully instruct and correct them as they learn this shot.

4. Once they learn the shot, teach them how to incorporate deception, since deception is vital to the success of this shot. Players should give off strong body and racquet signals to their opponent(s) that they will hit a topspin drive. At the last instant, the player leans back and hits the topspin lob. This deception freezes the opponent(s) at the net.

Forehand Slice Lobs

This is typically used as a defensive shot when stretched out wide to the forehand side without time to set up for a forehand topspin drive. Use this shot when

- stretched out wide on an ROS.
- hitting an ROS in doubles when you want to lob over the net player.
- your opponent is pressing the net, and you return a low ball that you cannot hit with a topspin lob to drive your opponent off the net.

If your players have mastered the technical aspects of this shot, skip this section.

1. Novice and intermediate players should start with a shortened continental grip. They use a forehand slice stroke, high to low, that is short and compact to send the ball high and deep with some backspin. Players should extend their grip length as they develop skill with this shot.

2. Have your players shadow drill this shot multiple times.

3. Hand toss balls to your players at the baseline. Carefully instruct and correct them as they learn this shot.

Backhand Slice Lobs

This is typically used as a defensive shot when stretched out wide to the backhand side without time to set up for a backhand topspin drive. Use this shot when

- stretched out wide on an ROS,
- hitting an ROS in doubles when you want to lob over the net player.
- your opponent is pressing the net, and you return a low ball that you cannot hit with a topspin lob to drive your opponent off the net.

If your players have mastered the technical aspects of this shot, skip this section.

1. Novice and intermediate players should start with a shortened continental grip. They use a backhand slice stroke, high to low, that is short and compact to send the ball high and deep with some backspin. Players should extend their grip length as they develop skill with this shot.

2. Have your players shadow drill this shot multiple times.

3. Hand toss balls to your players at the baseline. Carefully instruct and correct them as they learn this shot.

Overheads, a Dominant Way to End the Point

The ability to consistently hit winning overheads requires excellent technical skills and a calm, focused mental state.

If your players have mastered the technical aspects of this shot, skip this section.

1. Have players start with a short continental grip for better racquet and ball control.

2. Teach the 3 initial movements when the player recognizes an overhead opportunity:

   a. Turn 90 degrees to the net.

   b. Position the racquet in the cocked position.

   c. Extend the left arm, with the index finger pointing to the ball.

3. Stress the importance of excellent footwork while tracking the ball and getting to the optimal hitting position.

4. Have the players shadow drill this shot multiple times.

5. Hand toss or racquet toss balls up in the air near midcourt while standing nearby to observe players' technique. Have them hit overheads off the bounce only.

6. After several reps each of hitting the overhead off the bounce, allow players to choose to hit off the bounce or take the ball out of the air. Indicate to them

   • when it is best to hit the overhead off the bounce (a clear blue sky, significant wind, sun in the visual field, lack of confidence in hitting the overhead shot).

   • when it is reasonable to hit the overhead out of the air (cloudy background, slight or no wind, no sun problems, and confidence in hitting the overhead shot).

The Cooperative Topspin Lob, Overhead Game
The Setup

1. Assign 4 players to a court, playing 2 simultaneous 1 v 1 games, with a player in the middle of each service

box starting the points (with a hopper of balls between them) and a player at each half of the baseline.

2. The games are typically played cross-court, although they could be played straight ahead. Doubles players play on half the width of the doubles court; singles players play on half the width of the singles court or half the width of the doubles court.

3. The server gives the baseliner a reasonable underhand feed. The baseliner can hit topspin lobs only. The server can hit overheads or volleys, depending on the location and type of ball received. The server's job is to keep the ball in play by returning the lobs (or attempted lobs) back to the baseliner, who keeps hitting topspin lobs.

4. The coach calls time after 2–3 minutes, and the players rotate one spot. Continue the rotations until all players have hit from all 4 spots.

Coaching Tips and Players' Tips

This cooperative game gives players a high number of top-spin lob and overhead reps in a controlled setting. The coach may want to limit players to either forehand or back-hand topspin lobs during each complete rotation. With two full rotations, players get reps from both sides and are thus unable to avoid hitting this shot from their weaker side.

The Competitive Topspin Lob, Overhead Game
The Setup

1. Assign 4 players to a court, playing 2 simultaneous 1 v 1 games, with a player in the middle of each service box starting the point (with a hopper of balls between them) and a player at each half of the baseline.

2. The games are played cross-court and/or straight ahead. Doubles players play half the width of the doubles court; singles players play half the width of the singles court or half the width of the doubles court, per coach's decision.

3. The server gives the baseliner a reasonable underhand feed and keeps score. The baseliner can hit topspin lobs only, and the server can hit overheads or volleys, depending on the location and type of ball received.

4. The server cannot retreat behind the service line to hit any ball. If the lobber can hit a properly high and deep lob, he or she wins the point.

5. The coach calls time, or the players play to a specified point total. The winners and losers are declared, and the players rotate one spot until they have hit from all 4 spots.

Coaching Tips and Players' Tips

This competitive game works well if the players have at least some skill with both these shots. It puts realistic pressure on both the net player and the baseliner to hit precise shots.

An optional version of this game lets the server retreat behind the service line to hit any ball, which mimics an actual match situation.

The Cooperative Slice Lob, Overhead Game
The Setup

1. Assign 4 players to a court, playing 2 simultaneous 1 v 1 games, with a player in the middle of each service box starting the point (with a hopper of balls between them) and one player at each half of the baseline.

2. The games are played cross-court and/or straight ahead. Doubles players play on half the width of the doubles court, and singles players play on half the width of the singles court or on half the width of the doubles court, per coach's decision.

3. The server gives the baseliner a reasonable underhand feed, and the baseliner can hit slice lobs only. The server can hit overheads or volleys, depending on the location and type of ball received. The server's job is to keep the ball in play by returning the lobs (or

attempted lobs) back to the baseliner, who keeps hitting slice lobs.

4. The coach calls time, and the players rotate one spot, until they have hit from all 4 spots.

Coaching Tips and Players' Tips

This cooperative game gives players a high number of slice lob and overhead reps in a controlled setting. The coach may want to limit players to either forehand or backhand slice lobs during each complete rotation. With 2 full rotations, players get reps from both sides and are thus unable to avoid hitting this shot from their weaker side.

The Competitive Slice Lob, Overhead Game
The Setup

1. Assign 4 players to a court, playing 2 simultaneous 1 v 1 games, with a player in the middle of each service box starting the points (with a hopper of balls between them), and a player at each half of the baseline.

2. The games are played cross-court and/or straight ahead. Doubles players play on half the width of the doubles court, and singles players play on half the width of the singles court or half the width of the doubles court, per coach's decision.

3. The server gives the baseliner a reasonable underhand feed and keeps score. The baseliner can hit slice lobs only. The server can hit overheads or volleys, depending on the location and type of ball received.

4. The server cannot retreat behind the service line to hit any ball. If the lobber can hit a properly high and deep lob, he or she wins the point.

5. The coach calls time or the players play to a specified point total. Winners and losers are declared. Then the players rotate one spot, until they have hit from all 4 spots.

Coaching Tips and Players' Tips

This competitive game works well if the players have at least some skill with both these shots. It puts realistic pressure on both the net player and the baseliner to hit precise shots. The coach may choose to limit the baseliners to either forehand or backhand slice lobs in each complete rotation.

An optional version of this game lets the server retreat behind the service line to hit any ball, which mimics an actual match situation.

18 Training to Improve Strength and Conditioning

Strength is a crucial, sometimes overlooked element in tennis performance. Ambitious players invest time and energy in strength training. In this chapter, I detail some simple, inexpensive, and effective ways to improve physical strength that will definitely help your game.

Conditioning is an important element in singles matches that feature long rallies and extended battles during long two- and three-setters. What follows outlines some basic exercises to enhance your power and stamina.

Split-Step and Power-Skip Drill

This drill improves footwork, balance, leg power, stroke technique, and endurance.

The Setup

All steps are short and quick, integral to effective movement on the court. You do a split-step at every intersection of lines when following the described pattern. Each split-step is followed by a shadow stroke with a racquet, using the correct grip for the particular stroke being shadowed. If you do this on grass, match the same pattern you would use on a tennis court. A split-step training session lasts about 10–20 minutes.

1. On a tennis court, start at the right corner where the baseline and right singles sideline intersect. Move forward and split-step at the intersection of the service line and the right singles sideline, and do the shadow stroke.

   • Move to the left on the service line, split-step at the service line T, and do the shadow stroke.

   • Move backward, split-step on the baseline at the center hash mark, and do the shadow stroke.

   • Move left on the baseline, split-step at the intersection of the baseline and the left singles sideline, and do the shadow stroke.

   • Move forward on the left singles sideline, split-step at the intersection of the left singles sideline and the service line, and do the shadow stroke.

2. Power skip to the third court over if you are on a group of courts; if not, go a similar distance. Drive yourself as high as you can on each step. This plyometric exercise increases your first-step explosive power on the court.

3. Repeat the pattern of split-steps and shadow strokes as in step 1, but now go from left to right, doing the complement of your previous shadow stroke (such as the backhand volley after using the forehand volley).

4. Power skip to your starting position. You have completed one set.

5. Do multiple sets in a training session. Rest for 1 minute in between sets.

Coaching Tips

This is an excellent warm-up drill that accomplishes multiple objectives in one fell swoop. Players improve their footwork, their split-step, a chosen stroke, explosive leg power, balance, and conditioning. This drill does not include running, but it does include dynamic first steps, starts and stops, and short, quick steps. (Running has minimal value during practices, except for singles players who need excessive stamina for 2–3-hour matches in hot weather.) This drill practices most of the significant tennis movements, and it is important to remember that we are training our players to move better on the tennis court, not on the running track.

Players' Tips

If you are ambitious and willing to put in some training time outside of your regular lessons or practices, this training drill will help you become a stronger, more explosive, and more fit player on the court.

Shadow Drills with Your Racquet

This drill improves stroke technique, footwork, and balance.

The Setup

This drill can be done anywhere: on a tennis court, on a grassy area, in a basement, etc.

1. First do a correct split-step. Then visualize an incoming ball that you are going to hit. Take several short, quick steps in any direction. Then set up in proper position and use perfect technique while doing the shadow stroke. Do each stroke 5–10 times. Rest 10 seconds before moving on to the next stroke.

2. Do each of these strokes:
   - **Forehand topspin:** Use all three techniques (the pull-up, the classic, and the modern).
   - **Two-hand backhand topspin.**
   - **Forehand volleys and forehand slices:** Do high, medium, and low.
   - **Backhand volleys and backhand slices:** Do high, medium, and low.

- **Serves:** Do flat, slice, and topspin.
- **Overheads** (with footwork preceding this): Do both forehand and backhand.
- **Topspin lobs:** Do both forehand and backhand.
- **Slice lobs:** Do both forehand and backhand.
- **Drop shots:** Do both forehand and backhand.

Coaching Tips

If you ask your players to do shadow drills during practice sessions, you will probably meet with resistance from all but the most ambitious and compliant players. Suggest this to your players as an activity they can do on their own. The ambitious players will follow through and do this.

Players' Tips

If you are ambitious and you invest time performing shadow drills with your racquet, this will train your brain and muscles to "memorize" these movements, so you will produce smoother strokes.

Shadow Drills with a Light Hand Weight

This improves stroke technique as well as strength, footwork, and balance. This drill can be done anywhere: on a tennis court, on a grassy area, in a basement, etc.

The Setup

1. Use a light hand weight that you can handle easily, such as 2–5 pounds. Younger and weaker players should start with 2 pounds and gradually work up.

2. First do a correct split-step. Visualize an incoming ball that you are going to hit. Take several short, quick steps in any direction. Then set up in proper position and use perfect technique while doing the shadow stroke.

3. Do each stroke 5–10 times. Rest 10 seconds before moving on to the next stroke.

4. Do each of these strokes:

- **Forehand topspin:** Use all three techniques (the pull-up, the classic, and the modern).
- **Two-hand backhand topspin**
- **Forehand volleys and forehand slices:** Do high, medium, and low.
- **Backhand volleys and backhand slices:** Do high, medium, and low.
- **Serves:** Do flat, slice, and topspin.
- **Overheads** (with footwork preceding this): Do both forehand and backhand.
- **Topspin lobs:** Do both forehand and backhand.
- **Slice lobs:** Do both forehand and backhand.
- **Drop shots:** Do both forehand and backhand.

Coaching Tips

The shadow drills above with a light hand weight are awkward to do during a practice session because of the need for hand weights. Suggest to your players they do this drill at home; the ambitious ones will follow through.

Players' Tips

This drill gives you a simple and effective way to increase your hand, wrist, forearm, and shoulder strength, which will provide you with increased racquet control on the court.

A Weight Workout to Strengthen Hands, Wrists, Forearms, Upper Arms, and Shoulders

The Setup

1. Use two equal hand weights that are comfortable for you, such as 2–5 pounds each.

2. **Hand, wrist, and forearm exercises:** While sitting, rest your forearms on your thighs. Do 10–15 each of wrist flexions, wrist extensions, and sideways flexion-extensions.

3. **Biceps curls:** While sitting or standing, do 10–15 each of biceps curls with the palms in 3 positions: palm down, palm sideways, and palm up.

4. **Shoulder exercises:** With your arms at your sides, raise them up until the weights touch directly overhead. Extend the weights behind your shoulders allowing the elbows to bend, then raise them directly overhead. Repeat 10–15 times.

5. **Overhead presses:** Hold a weight in each hand, on each side of your head, at shoulder height, and then raise the weights vertically to full arm extension. Repeat 10–15 times.

Grip Exercises

These exercises improve grip strength and endurance. You need one or two grip exercisers.

The Setup

1. Do 5–10 reps for each hand. Rest for 10 seconds in between. Do multiple sets.

2. If you have 2 grip exercisers, do both hands simultaneously.

The Balance Drill

This improves overall balance and proprioception (use of nerves and muscles to maintain your position in space). It may help prevent devastating anterior cruciate ligament (ACL) tears of the knee and significant ankle injuries.

The Setup

1. Stand on your right foot. Do a selected shadow stroke repeatedly with your racquet for 30 seconds.

2. Repeat step 1 with your eyes closed.

3. Stand on your left foot. Do a selected shadow stroke repeatedly with your racquet for 30 seconds.

4. Repeat step 3 with your eyes closed.

Sprinting

This improves speed, footwork, and short-burst tennis conditioning.

The Setup

1. Do short sprints of about 20 yards, preferably on grass to avoid impact injuries (such as stress fractures of the feet and legs).
2. Do sets of 5–10 of each type of sprint: forward, backward, to the left, to the right.
3. Walk back to the starting point after each sprint.

Footwork and Leg Power Drills

These drills improve foot movement coordination, agility, balance, leg strength, and stroke mechanics. They work beautifully going from the baseline to the net and back, but any similar distance will suffice. Several or all of these drills can be done as part of a pre-practice warm-up. If these drills are done as a training session by ambitious players, do them continuously for 10–20 minutes.

The Setup

1. Face the net. Do crossover steps going from the baseline to the net and quick back-shuffle steps to return.
2. Face a sideline, standing sideways to the net. Side shuffle to the net. Facing the same direction, side shuffle to return.
3. Face a sideline, standing sideways to the net. Do crossover steps to the net. Facing the same direction, do cross-over steps to return.
4. Pointing the feet outward 20-30 degrees, do slow lunge steps, bending the knees to 90 degrees. Return with quick back-shuffle steps.
5. With feet together, do side-to-side hops to the net. Return with quick back-shuffle steps.

6. Power skip to the net. Return with quick back-shuffle steps.

7. Take 2 steps toward the net, then do a split-step and shadow drill a stroke. Repeat this pattern until you reach the net. Return doing the same movements.

Coaching Tips

Tell your players that these training drills will improve their on-court strength and conditioning and, by extension, their on-court performance. Teach them how to do these exercises. Some of your ambitious players will no doubt put in extra time to improve.

Players' Tips

Learn to do some or all of these exercises. Purchase some inexpensive hand weights, budget some time and energy to do these drills, and realize that this mostly off-court training will enhance your on-court performance for a small investment of time and money.

19 Tennis Parents: Advice to Consider and Some Key Dos and Don'ts

have been a tennis parent three times over, with three kids who developed an interest in tennis at around age 11 or 12 and who pursued the sport with varying levels of intensity and passion. All three played in junior tournaments as well as high school tennis for 4 years, with a certain degree of success. As I watched our kids win some big matches and lose some big matches, I went through the tennis parent emotional roller-coasters that are guaranteed to occur.

This chapter discusses some important topics for the tennis parent: early stages of your child's tennis journey; middle and later stages of your child's tennis journey; key parental dos and don'ts; and match anxiety.

Early Stages of Your Child's Tennis Journey

This section delineates some observations and thoughts I have regarding what you, as a tennis parent, should think about and do as you prepare to start (or have already started) the tennis journey with your child. Typically, it is a parent or a close relative/friend who introduces a child to tennis.

I divide tennis parents into three groups: those who have never played tennis, those who casually play the game, and those who are avid/advanced players. It is definitely true that each parent's tennis background significantly affects that parent's viewpoints and decisions.

For the Nonplaying Tennis Parent

Your child may enjoy the game purely because it is a positive social experience now. Tennis can also be enjoyed as a life-long sport.

The game provides moderate to high-level exercise for kids, which can only be a positive in this age of computer, TV, cell phone, iPod, and video game sedentary pursuits. Childhood and adult obesity rates are clearly increasing, and it is in your child's best short-term and long-term interest to pursue some type of vigorous physical activity.

Tennis is a complex game, as your child will learn through practices, lessons, clinics, hitting with friends, matches, tournaments, etc. It is a good idea for you to learn about the game as well, so that you can understand what you are watching and enjoy some of the complex aspects. If you read all or parts of this book you will begin to understand the game of tennis and its vocabulary

For the Tennis Parent Who Is a Casual Player

If your child learns and enjoys the game, you may have a common activity to participate in with your child now and for years in the future, which may be a particularly precious commodity during the tumultuous teenage years.

If your child grows passionate about the game and wants to improve to play at intermediate or advanced levels, it may stimulate you to take steps to improve your game.

For the Tennis Parent Who Is an Avid/Advanced Player

You absolutely want your child to learn tennis and to love it as much as you do. Can you encourage this without messing up and turning your child against the sport you are so passionate about? This takes a high level of self-discipline and restraint on your part. When you introduce your child to tennis, avoid insisting that he or she pursue and love the sport. This is a delicate dance that you must do with care and consideration.

You must be willing to let your child pursue other interests if tennis is not the activity that captures his or her passion. If you push, you will have a battle over this wonderful game, and most likely the outcome will not be to your liking.

Remember: What your child is enthralled with at age 6 or 9 or 12 or 15 may be fleeting. If your child detests tennis at age 9, perhaps at age 12 the interest will arise, or maybe it will emerge at age 25 or age 40.

If your child is in love with tennis at age 10, perhaps at age 14 another, more important pursuit will emerge. You as the tennis parent must adapt to these changes, because it is your child playing the game, not you.

Middle and Later Stages of Your Child's Tennis Journey

This section examines some scenarios that could arise as your child develops his or her tennis skills.

For the Nonplaying Tennis Parent, Consider These Scenarios

1. You note that your child has moderate athletic skills and now has developed moderate tennis skills. Your child is interested in more training opportunities: private lessons, small group lessons, tennis camps, and tennis clinics. You know that each of these endeavors will require effort to arrange, will be expensive, and will require transportation time and expense. You are not sure what value these activities will have.

   My recommendation: Seek out a knowledgeable, experienced tennis coach or instructor. Ask for advice regarding what might be helpful for your child's tennis development and what might be reasonable in terms of your investment of time and money.

2. You arrange for your child to take private lessons on tennis fundamentals, drive your child to the lesson site, watch the lesson, and pay the fee. What do you derive from this?

   Consider this: Perhaps you could take the same lessons on fundamentals with your child, if your child and the instructor agree. Then you will be on the court with your child, sharing an activity that you are learning together. Instead of being a passive observer/transporter/fee payer, you become an active participant in the wonderful journey of acquiring tennis knowledge and skill.

3. You drive your child to a tournament and you watch the matches, but you really do not understand what you are seeing.

   My advice: Selectively read this book to familiarize yourself with tennis language. If you know some of the terms and talk to other tennis parents, you will have opportunities to ask questions and start to tune into what is happening on the court. In addition, consider taking a lesson or two, or talk your child into going to a court and teaching you a few things that he or she has been learning.

For the Tennis Parent Who Is a Casual Player, Consider These Scenarios

1. Your child has taken a few lessons, and when you hit with your child, you realize your child uses different grips and stroke techniques than you do. You are puzzled by this.

   Consider this: Ask your child to explain what he or she is doing and learn from that. In addition, if you can arrange it with an instructor, consider taking some lessons with your child so you can learn about correct grips and stroke techniques at the same time as your child.

2. Your child, now a young teen, can easily out-hit and outrun you on the court.

   Possible approach: Using this book as a guide, select some small-segment competitive training games to use when on the court with your child. This limits the differential in court coverage and may allow you to have an enjoyable experience together. Alternatively, use some of the cooperative training games from this book, which removes the competitive aspect.

For the Tennis Parent Who Is an Avid/Advanced Player, Consider These Scenarios

1. Your young teen is now a midlevel player, and you want to see your child play in more tournaments and take more lessons so he or she will move up to the advanced level.

   My advice: Be careful how you approach this aspect of tennis with your child. Teens may decide, sometimes impulsively, that they no longer want to be involved in some activity. This is more likely to happen if the parent pressures the teen to up the ante in terms of commitment.

   It may be best to quietly and subtly mention some options that you would like your child to consider. Then be patient and wait for your child to express an interest.

2. Your young teen is now a midlevel player, and you want to get on the court with him or her frequently, so you can help your teen get in the repetitions he or she needs to become an advanced player.

   Remember: Your teen has intense desires to fit in with peers, and being seen on a tennis court with a parent may not be the ideal scenario for him or her. You may be more successful if you ask your teen to hit on a court at a time when no teen friend is likely to be an observer.

   Also remember: At some point—usually sooner than you might imagine—your teen may not want to relate to you as his or her coach. If you hit together and suggest some improvements regarding techniques or tactics and your teen gives you the clear message that he or she is not interested, be smart. Drop the suggestions completely and hit for fun and exercise. Leave the coaching to someone else.

Before our son's high school sophomore tennis season, I contacted his head coach, whom I knew well, and asked if he might be interested in me becoming a volunteer assistant coach with the team. After the coach gave his approval, I told our son about this development. His response was, "Fine, dad, you coach, and I won't play!"

Needless to say, I did not expect this response. I was stunned. I assured our son that I would not work with him in practice, and that I would not be involved in coaching him during any of his matches (which was the agreed-upon plan with the head coach). Two months passed and the season was about to start. I asked our son if he could tolerate me being a volunteer assistant coach if I was not involved with coaching him in any way. He reluctantly agreed to this.

This arrangement worked beautifully. During practice sessions and matches, our son was coached by the head coach, while I worked with other players. However, one day during our son's junior season, the head coach asked me to spend an hour doing drills with 6 players, including our son. After the long 60 minutes was over, it was abundantly clear that this was a one-time event, never to be repeated—and it was not.

Key Dos and Don'ts for Tennis Parents

- **Do** give your child positive encouragement, even if he or she is the least skilled in the group lessons, and even if he or she loses every match in every dual and every tournament entered. Remember, if your child likes tennis enough to persevere despite these outcomes, it is important to him or her, and you must recognize and respect that.

- **Do** practice patience during your child's tennis development. Kids develop at wildly different rates and stages. Tennis players need a certain level of strength, visual and spatial perception, and motor coordination to be reasonably proficient. Some kids develop these important qualities much earlier and more quickly than others, but the laggards at one age may become the leaders later.

- **Don't** say a single negative word to your child during or after a tennis match, especially after a loss. Negative words at this time do not accomplish one iota of good, and they may create a major chasm between you and your child.

- **Don't** make any comments to your child during a lesson or a practice unless you are on the court taking the lesson with your child. This is a time for your child to be directed by an instructor or coach, and your child needs to develop a relationship with that person on his or her own terms.

- **Do** talk directly to your child's coach if you are unhappy about your child's position on the team (JV vs. varsity, singles vs. doubles, #1 vs. #3 singles, etc.). Simmering discontent on the part of a parent (or parents) on the sidelines is a true negative for all parties. Arrange to meet with the coach as soon as possible to engage in an honest, open discussion about your thoughts and feelings. You and the coach will have the opportunity to exchange observations and opinions, and hopefully, come to an agreeable conclusion.

- **Do** give your child a few carefully selected words of encouragement during matches—if that is acceptable to your child—such as "nice shot," "great effort," "good serve." If your child makes it crystal clear that hearing your voice during a match is a distraction or worse, then move far enough away and whisper so that your child cannot possibly hear what you say. Using this tactic, you will have the satisfaction of verbally supporting your child, yet avoid being an irritating parent.

- **Don't** ever belittle your child's opponent during a match and don't ever cheer for an opponent's error. It is immature, unkind, and the wrong thing to do.

- **Do** applaud your child's opponent's excellent shot or hustle or serve. It is the mature and the right thing to do.

- **Don't** attempt to give your child coaching advice during a match. It is contrary to good tennis etiquette, and it is contrary to good common sense. If your child is at a tournament without a coach, it is a wonderful opportunity for your child to independently face challenges and solve problems. If your child is playing a match with a school coach present, leave the coaching role to the official coach.

- **Do** understand that nearly all tennis players make a good faith effort to call line calls correctly. Typically players have heard this message numerous times from their coach or instructor. This unique aspect of tennis—trusting your opponent to call line calls honestly—is an integral part of the game.

- **Don't** comment on line calls that you do not like. Tennis rules require the players to question line calls they disagree with. It is the players who must ask for a line judge if they repeatedly question line calls.

- **Don't** spend a large sum of money on a tennis racquet for your novice player. A $30–80 racquet will suffice while your child gets some tennis experience and decides whether to pursue the game in earnest. A $200 dollar racquet that is used a few times, then relegated to the back of a closet, will be a reminder of a tennis parent's dream that has dissipated.

- **Do** obtain expert advice on buying a suitable racquet with the correct grip size for your child. A suitable racquet with the correct grip size does make a difference in racquet control, ball control, and performance.

- **Do** ask the advice of a coach or instructor regarding purchasing a more expensive racquet and high-end strings if your child is a devoted player and is pursuing the game with dedication.

- **Do** occasionally ask your child's coach or instructor about your child's progress. This helps you maintain a relationship with the coach/instructor (most coaches and instructors will be pleased to give you a progress report), and keeps you informed as to what is happening with your child on the tennis court.

- **Don't** brag about or broadcast the fact that your child, blessed with rare athletic gifts and the recipient of years of tennis training, is a big-time winner. No one (except perhaps a grandparent) wants to hear this information unless they ask first.

Match Anxiety

Match anxiety is sure to occur as you, the tennis parent, watch your child compete in a close match. When it happens, try to recognize it right away. You can develop coping strategies to keep this anxiety at a tolerable level. I am going to detail a few thoughts and experiences that I have had and observations I have made as examples of how parents might cope with match anxiety.

Several years ago, our son played in a number of junior tournaments, and I got to know the mother of another boy who played in the same events. She related to me her severe, unremitting match anxiety when her son was on the court. I gave her my perspective: that I was thankful our son was healthy and chose to spend his time and energy competing on a tennis court rather than playing video games, watching TV, or pursuing drug experiences. That is what helped me keep winning and losing in perspective.

When our oldest daughter was competing in an important high school tournament match that developed into a long, close three-setter, I found myself gradually moving away from her court, until I was in a position about two courts away. From that spot, I found I could watch the match with less anxiety. Several years later, I had the same experience watching our youngest daughter playing a gut-wrenching three-setter. I have witnessed many parents do the same thing, typically finding a spot a few courts away from their child, to watch an ongoing match. This coping mechanism is simple, and allows each anxious parent to adjust the distance from their child's court to keep their anxiety at a tolerable level.

A coping mechanism some players use (and we coaches encourage it) may be beneficial for some parents. Players who focus on the score of the match can benefit by changing their focus to each individual point and the excitement and pleasure of playing that point, rather than dwelling on the previous point or previous game or the score or what the score could or should be. Parents, if you focus on each point and the shots every player (not only your child) on the court makes during the point, and the effort and energy expended by every player on the court, you may be able to appreciate the skill and athleticism you are witnessing and applaud that, rather than obsessing over your child's performance and the outcome of the match.

20 The Pursuit of Tennis Excellence Is Serious—But Keep It Fun

The preceding chapters feature a major amount of serious tennis training information.

As coaches, we need this serious information and knowledge so we can help our players advance their skills and their match play performances.

As players, we need this serious work so we can compete more successfully in junior tournaments or in high school matches, or as 3.0 or 3.5 league players, and perhaps move up to that coveted 4.0 rating.

As tennis parents, we need to understand all of the serious learning and training time our children experience as they travel their tennis journey.

In a high-stakes situation, you may be coaching in a match that will determine the conference championship, or playing in an adult league match that will determine who will go to the state playoffs, or watching your child play in an important junior tournament match, or a high school JV or varsity match.

Remember this: Tennis is certainly an intriguing, intricate, fascinating game, but it is best to avoid obsessing over winning the game, because that surely leads to emotions such as dread, anger, humiliation, and disappointment. In contrast, in emergency medicine, I and other emergency medicine physicians, emergency nurses, and other emergency personnel must obsess over doing everything exactly right so our patients will have an opportunity to win the game they are engaged in.

As a closing thought, I proclaim that it is a reasonably healthy and sane thing to be enthralled with the game of tennis. If we are coaching and playing and parenting within the rules and within the spirit of the game, to the best of our abilities, we can repeatedly experience the joys and treasures of competition between the lines.

DEC 2017

UNION COUNTY PUBLIC LIBRARY
316 E. Windsor St., Monroe, NC 28112

CPSIA information can be obtained
at www.ICGtesting.com
Printed in the USA
LVOW04s2003231117

557331LV00005B/215/P